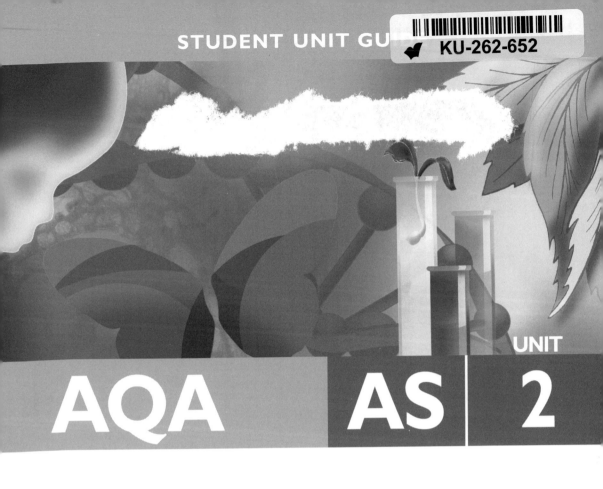

STUDENT UNIT GUIDE

UNIT

AQA   AS   2

Biology

The Variety of Living Organisms

Steve Potter

Philip Allan Updates, an imprint of Hodder Education, an Hachette UK Company, Market Place, Deddington, Oxfordshire OX15 0SE

Orders

Bookpoint Ltd, 130 Milton Park, Abingdon, Oxfordshire OX14 4SB
tel: 01235 827720
fax: 01235 400454
e-mail: uk.orders@bookpoint.co.uk
Lines are open 9.00 a.m.–5.00 p.m., Monday to Saturday, with a 24-hour message answering service. You can also order through the Philip Allan Updates website: www.philipallan.co.uk

© Philip Allan Updates 2009

ISBN 978-0-340-94951-1

First printed 2009
Impression number 5 4 3
Year 2014 2013 2012 2011 2010 2009

This guide has been written specifically to support students preparing for the AQA AS Biology Unit 2 examination. The content has been neither approved nor endorsed by AQA and remains the sole responsibility of the author.

Printed by MPG Books, Bodmin

Hachette UK's policy is to use papers that are natural, renewable and recyclable products and made from wood grown in sustainable forests. The logging and manufacturing processes are expected to conform to the environmental regulations of the country of origin.

Contents

Introduction

■ ■ ■

Content Guidance

■ ■ ■

Questions and Answers

Introduction

About this guide

This guide is written to help you to prepare for the Unit 2 examination of the new AQA Biology specification. Unit 2 examines the content of **Unit 2: The Variety of Living Organisms**, and forms part of the AS assessment; it will also contribute to the A2 assessment. Some of the material may be re-examined in synoptic questions in A2 examinations.

This **Introduction** provides guidance on revision, together with advice on approaching the unit examination.

The **Content Guidance** section gives a point-by-point description of all the facts you need to know and concepts you need to understand for Unit 2. In each topic, the concepts are presented first. It is a good idea to get your mind around these key ideas before you try to learn all the associated facts.

The **Question and Answer** section shows you the sorts of questions you can expect in the unit examination. It would be impossible to give examples of every kind of question in one book, but these should give you a flavour of what to expect. Each question has been attempted by two candidates, Candidate A and Candidate B. Their answers, along with the examiner's comments, should help you to see what you need to do to score a good mark — and how you can easily *not* score a mark even though you probably understand the biology.

What can I assume about the guide?

You *can* assume that:
- the basic facts you need to know and understand are stated explicitly
- the major concepts you need to understand are explained clearly
- the questions at the end of the guide are similar in style to those that will appear in the end-of-unit examination
- the answers supplied are the answers of AS students
- the standard of the marking is broadly equivalent to that which will be applied to your answers

What can I not assume about the guide?

You *must not* assume that:
- the diagrams used will be the same as those used in the end-of-unit examination (they may be more or less detailed, seen from a different angle etc.)
- the way in which the concepts are explained is the *only* way in which they can be presented in an examination (concepts are often presented in an unfamiliar situation)
- the range of question types presented is exhaustive (examiners are always thinking of new ways to test a topic)

How Science Works

This is a new component in the biology specifications of all examination boards. The aim is to help you to understand the *process* of scientific work. You will not find any specific section devoted to 'How Science Works' (HSW) in this guide, but the main aspects of HSW are described below:

- Scientists use pre-existing knowledge and understanding/theories/models to suggest explanations for phenomena.
- They design, carry out, analyse and evaluate scientific investigations to test new explanations.
- They share their findings with other scientists so that they may (or not) be validated.

As a consequence of the work of scientists, there may be implications for society as a whole. You are expected to appreciate and make informed (not emotional) comment on such aspects as:

- the ethical implications of the way in which research is carried out
- the way in which society uses science to help in decision making

Some of the questions in the Question and Answer section address HSW.

So how should I use this guide?

The guide lends itself to a number of uses throughout your course — it is not *just* a revision aid. You could:

- use it to check that your notes cover the material required by the specification
- use it to identify your strengths and weaknesses
- use it as a reference for homework and internal tests
- use it during your revision to prepare 'bite-sized' chunks of related material, rather than being faced with a file full of notes

The Questions and Answers section could be used to:

- identify the terms used by examiners in questions and what they expect of you
- familiarise yourself with the style of questions you can expect
- identify the ways in which marks are lost as well as how they are gained

Preparing for the Unit 2 examination

Preparation for examinations is a very personal thing. Different people prepare, equally successfully, in very different ways. The key is being totally honest about what actually *works* for you.

Whatever your style, you must have a plan. Sitting down the night before the examination with a file full of notes and a textbook does not constitute a revision plan — it is just desperation — and you must not expect a great deal from it. Whatever your personal style, there are a number of things you *must* do and a number of other things you *could* do.

Things you *must* do

- Leave yourself enough time to cover all the material.
- Make sure that you have all the material to hand (use this book as a basis).
- Identify weaknesses early in your preparation so that you have time to do something about them.
- Familiarise yourself with the terminology used in examination questions (see below).

Things you *could* do to help you learn

Psychologists have shown that you learn facts and ideas better if you are *active* in your learning. Just reading your notes over and over again is not a good way of revising. Instead, you could:

- write a summary of your notes that includes all the key points
- write key points on postcards (carry them around with you for a quick revise during a coffee break)
- discuss a topic with a friend who is studying the same course
- try to explain a topic to someone not on the course
- practise examination questions on the topic

All of these techniques make you *think* about the material. The more you process the information as you revise, the more effective your revision will be.

Approaching the end-of-unit examination

Terms used in examination questions

You will be asked precise questions in the examinations, so you can save valuable time and ensure that you score as many marks as possible by knowing what is expected. Terms most commonly used are explained below.

- Describe — this means exactly what it says ('tell me about...') and you should not need to explain why.
- Explain — give biological reasons for *why* or *how* something is happening.
- Complete — finish off a diagram, graph, flow chart or table.
- Draw/plot — construct some type of graph. For this, make sure that you:
  - choose a scale that makes good use of the graph paper (if a scale is not given) and does not leave all the plots tucked away in one corner
  - plot an appropriate type of graph — if both variables are continuous variables, then a line graph is usually the most appropriate; if one is a discrete variable, then a bar chart is appropriate
  - plot carefully using a sharp pencil and draw lines accurately
- From the... — use only information in the diagram/graph/photograph or other form of data.
- Name — give the name of a structure/molecule/organism etc.

- Suggest — i.e. 'give a plausible biological explanation for' — this term is often used when testing understanding of concepts in an unfamiliar situation.
- Compare — give similarities and differences between...
- Calculate — add, subtract, multiply, divide (do some kind of sum!) and show how you got your answer — *always* show your working!

The examination

When you finally open the test paper, it can be quite a stressful moment. You may not recognise the diagram or graph used in question 1. It can be quite demoralising to attempt a question at the start of an examination if you are not feeling confident about it. The following advice should help you to achieve a good result.

- Do *not* begin to write as soon as you open the paper.
- Do *not* necessarily answer question 1 first, just because it is printed first (the examiner did not sequence the questions with your particular favourites in mind).
- Scan *all* the questions before you begin to answer any.
- Identify those questions about which you feel most confident.
- *Answer first* those questions about which you feel most confident, regardless of the order in the paper.
- *Read the question carefully* — if you are asked to explain, then explain, don't just describe.
- Take notice of the mark allocation. Don't supply the examiner with all your knowledge of osmosis if there is only 1 mark allocated (similarly, you have to come up with four ideas if 4 marks are allocated).
- Try to stick to the point in your answer (it is easy to stray into related areas that will not score marks and which will use up valuable time).
- Take particular care with:
  – drawings — you will not be asked to produce complex diagrams, but those you do produce must resemble the subject
  – labelling — label lines *must* touch the part you are required to identify; if they stop short or pass through the part, you will lose marks
  – graphs — draw *small* points if you are asked to plot a graph and join the plots with ruled lines or, if specifically asked for, a line or smooth curve of best fit through all the plots
- Try to answer *all* the questions.

Content
Guidance

This section is a guide to the content of **Unit 2: The Variety of Living Organisms**. The main areas of this unit are:

- the nature of variation
- DNA — its structure and how it works
- passing on the genetic material
- the genetic diversity of populations
- selection in a population
- different sized organisms
- different cells in different organisms
- different molecules in different organisms
- classifying organisms
- biodiversity

Key facts you must know and understand

These are exactly what you might think: a summary of all the basic knowledge that you must be able to recall and show that you understand. The knowledge has been broken down into a number of small facts that you must learn. This means that the list of 'Key facts' for some topics is quite long. However, this approach makes quite clear *everything* you need to know about the topic.

Key concepts you must understand

These are a little different. Whereas you can learn facts, these are ideas or concepts that often form the basis of models that we use to explain aspects of biology. You can know the words that describe a concept like osmosis, or resolving power of a microscope, but you will not be able to use this information unless you really understand what is going on. Once you genuinely understand a concept, you will probably not have to learn it again.

What the examiners could ask you to do

This part will try to give you an insight into the minds of the examiners who will set and mark your examination papers. They may ask you to recall any of the basic knowledge or explain any of the key concepts; but they may well do more than that. Examiners think up questions where the concepts you understand are in a different setting or context from the one(s) you are familiar with. This could include the evaluation of data under the 'How Science Works' requirement, set in the context of this particular topic.

Bear in mind that examiners will often set individual questions that involve knowledge and understanding of more than one section. The sample questions in the Question and Answer section of this book will help you to practise drawing together material from different areas of the specification.

The nature of variation

Key concepts you must understand

The variation within a species is called **intraspecific variation**; that between different species is **interspecific variation**.

Intraspecific variation can be caused by:
- genetic differences
- differences in the environment
- a combination of genetic and environmental influences

A **species** is a group of individuals that are similar physically and physiologically and which can interbreed to produce fertile offspring.

A **population** is the total number of organisms of one species in a given area at a given time.

A **sample** is a subset of a population.

Continuous variation is variation in which there is a continuous range of values, such as in human height and body mass. **Categoric (discontinuous) variation** is variation in which only a limited number of discrete (separate) categories are possible, for example, number of teeth.

Continuously variable features are often **normally distributed**; their variability can be described by the **mean** and the **standard deviation**.

A **gene** is a section of DNA that controls a particular feature (e.g. eye colour); an **allele** is one particular version of a gene (e.g. blue or brown alleles of the gene for eye colour).

Key facts you must know and understand

No two organisms are identical; there is always some difference. There are fewer differences between different humans than between humans and other animals. Humans are all members of the same species — *Homo sapiens*. In other words, the extent of intraspecific variation is usually less than the extent of interspecific variation.

Genetic variation can be a result of different genes or different alleles of the same genes, brought about by:
- mutations
- crossing-over in meiosis (see pages 27–28)
- independent assortment of chromosomes in meiosis (see pages 27–28)
- random fertilisation of gametes (any male gamete could fertilise any available female gamete)

Organisms with the same genes may still be slightly different due to the effects of the environment. At birth, identical twins are never quite the same; they occupied different positions in the womb and probably had different sized placentas. As a result, one may have received more nutrients than the other and so was born heavier. The flowers of genetically identical hydrangea plants can differ in colour, depending on the pH of the soil (pink in low pH, blue in higher pH).

Tall pea plants are taller than dwarf pea plants because of different alleles of the gene for height, but all tall pea plants are not the same height because of differences in the environment (they may receive different amounts of water, mineral ions, light etc., which affect their growth). So variation in the height of pea plants is due to a combination of genetic and environmental effects. This is illustrated in Figure 1.

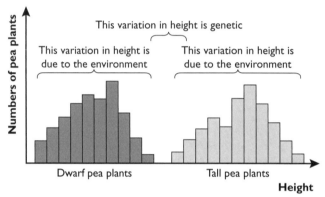

Figure 1 Genetic and environmental variation of height in pea plants

Features showing categoric (discontinuous) variation present an 'either/or' situation — there are a limited number of variants or different categories. For example, blood groups and eye colour.

Features showing continuous variation show an uninterrupted range of different types. For example, height in humans, body mass in humans and leaf width in pea plants.

The frequencies of each type in a population can be shown in graphs. We plot a **bar chart** to show categoric variation but a **histogram** to show continuous variation.

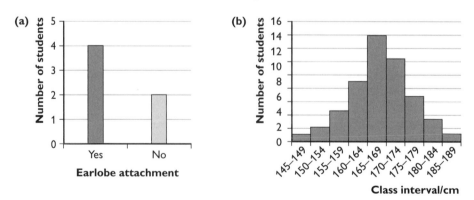

Figure 2 (a) A bar chart of earlobe attachment and (b) a histogram of height in 17-year-old students

> **Tip** Make sure that you know when to plot a bar chart and when to plot a histogram. Basically, if the variable is of the 'either/or' kind (categoric), you will plot a bar chart and *the bars won't touch*. If the variable is continuous, you plot a histogram *with touching bars*.

Measuring the variation in a population involves taking a sample of that population — it would be impractical to try to measure every single member of the population. The sample should be a **random sample** to avoid any **bias** in the choosing of individuals. If the sample is large enough, it will probably be quite representative of the whole population, but small samples can easily be unrepresentative.

If enough values are plotted of a feature showing continuous variation, the distribution of heights forms a bell-shaped curve, called a **normal distribution curve**.

A normal distribution can be described mathematically by two features of the curve:
- The **mean** ($\bar{x}$) is the sum of all the values divided by the total number of individuals.
- The **standard deviation** (σ) is the portion of the curve that includes 34% of all values above the mean or below the mean.

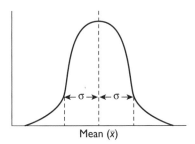

Mean ($\bar{x}$)

Figure 3 The mean and standard deviation of a typical normal distribution

The mean is a measure of 'central tendency' — it tells you the 'typical value'. The standard deviation is a measure of 'dispersion' — it tells you the extent to which the data are spread about the mean.

The standard deviation is more useful in this respect than just looking at the overall **range** of values. The range is defined solely by the two extreme values; it does not matter where the intervening values lie or how many of them there are. The values at the extremes can easily be 'freakish' — a long way removed from the next nearest values. We call these **outliers** and they distort the impression of the variability of the feature.

However, the standard deviation takes into account the extent of the difference of each and every value from the mean.

The two normal distributions below have the same mean, but have very different standard deviations. Population (a) shows much more variability than population (b), and this is reflected in their standard deviations.

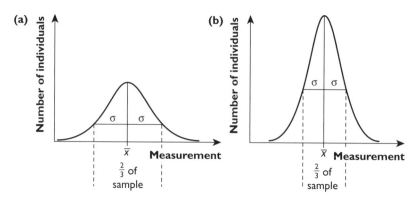

Figure 4 Standard deviation

HSW The tentative nature of experimental results

When presenting the results of their research, scientists try to show something of the degree of uncertainty in the data. One way of doing this is to repeat their experiments many times and calculate the mean and standard deviation of these results. The standard deviation can be used to calculate another value called the standard error, and the value of the standard error is often shown on graphs as 'error bars' to illustrate the range of results for a given condition. If error bars for two different conditions overlap, it suggests that there may not be a significant difference between the two. If the error bars don't overlap, then the results suggest a real difference between the two. But even then, it is not certain.

Figure 5 shows the effect of two diets on the concentration of glycogen in the muscles of men and women.

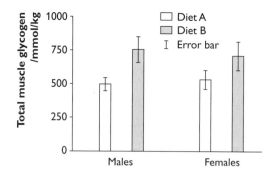

Figure 5 Concentration of glycogen in the muscles of men and women

The error bars show that, in males, there is a significant difference between the two diets, but that this is not the case in females. The error bars also show that, for each diet, there is no significant difference between males and females.

What the examiners could ask you to do

- Explain any of the key concepts.
- Recall and show understanding of any of the key facts.
- Interpret data in graphs/tables and identify whether continuous or discontinuous variation is shown.
- Interpret data showing variation in results, describe any trends shown and suggest causes of the variation.
- Comment on the variability of data.

DNA — its structure and how it works

Key concepts you must understand

DNA is the molecule of inheritance; it is a huge molecule made from two strands wound into a double helix.

One of these strands is called the **coding strand**; this strand carries the code for specific features. The other strand does not carry any code and is called the **non-coding strand.**

It is a stable molecule; this is essential so that genetic information passed on in cell divisions is consistent from one generation of cells to the next.

It also ensures that the genetic information is consistent from one generation of individuals to the next.

Sections of the DNA molecule are called genes; each gene is a part of the coding strand and controls the development of one feature.

A gene controls a feature by coding for a protein that directly or indirectly determines that feature.

The genes code for proteins by means of triplets of organic bases on the coding strand of the DNA molecule, which code for an amino acid in the protein molecule; it is, therefore, a **triplet code**.

This 'genetic code' is a **universal code** — it is the same in bacteria, penguins, humans, bananas and all other living organisms.

The genetic code is a **degenerate code**; there are 64 triplets that code for only twenty amino acids, so most amino acids have more than one code.

Because of its size, DNA cannot leave the nucleus and so must produce a 'messenger' to direct the cell to synthesise proteins; this molecule is called **messenger RNA (mRNA)**.

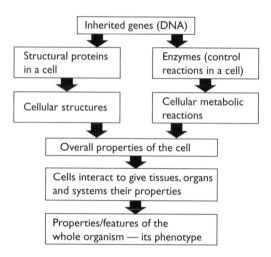

Figure 6 Genes affect the whole organism

DNA contains non-coding regions, both within genes (called introns) and between genes (called **minisatellites** and **microsatellites**).

Key facts you must know and understand

The structure of DNA

DNA is made of two strands wound into a double helix. Each strand is made from many structures called nucleotides; it is a **polynucleotide**.

Each DNA nucleotide is made up of:
- an organic, nitrogenous base (either **adenine**, **thymine**, **cytosine** or **guanine**)
- a molecule of **deoxyribose** (a pentose sugar — a sugar with five carbon atoms)
- a phosphate group

The two strands are arranged in a precise manner, shown in the diagrams below.

A nucleotide containing the base adenine on one of the strands is *always* paired with one containing thymine on the other strand. A nucleotide containing the base cytosine is always paired with one containing guanine. This is the **base-pairing rule**. Adenine and thymine are said to be **complementary bases**, as are cytosine and guanine.

The size of a DNA molecule is described in terms of the numbers of base pairs it contains. Because there are so many, these units are often kilobase pairs (thousands of base pairs) or megabase pairs (millions of base pairs).

The strands are oriented opposite to each other. The 'start' or 'top' of one strand is paired with the 'end' or 'bottom' of the other. The two strands are said to be **anti-parallel**.

The covalent bonds holding the nucleotides together in each strand are stronger than the hydrogen bonds holding the two strands together. The strong covalent bonds

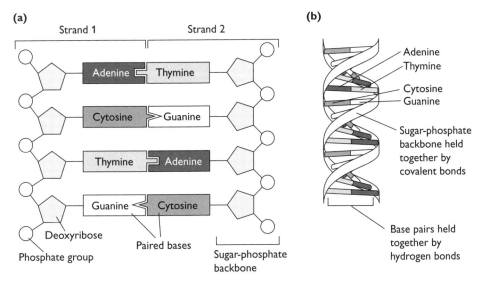

Figure 7 (a) DNA comprises base pairs attached to a sugar-phosphate backbone and (b) formed into a double helix

ensure that the structure of each strand is stable. The hydrogen bonds are much weaker and this allows the two strands to be separated easily. This is important in replication of the DNA (see page 23) and in protein synthesis (see pages 18–19).

> **Tip** You may be given information about the percentage of one base in a sample of DNA and asked to calculate the percentage of any or all of the other bases. It is very easy if you remember that:
> - % adenine + % cytosine or % guanine = 50
> - % thymine + % cytosine or % guanine = 50
> Or, putting it in general terms:
> - % of known base + % of either of the non-complementary bases = 50
> - % of any base = % of its complementary base

Size, location and organisation of DNA in eukaryotic and prokaryotic cells

Feature of DNA	Eukaryotic cell	Prokaryotic cell
Size of molecule	10^8–10^9 base pairs (100–1000 megabase pairs)	10^5–10^6 base pairs (0.1–10 megabase pairs)
Nature of molecule	Linear Associated with histone proteins to form **chromosomes**	Circular Naked (not associated with histone proteins) Some DNA exists as very small, circular **plasmids**
Location of molecule	In nucleus	Free in cytoplasm

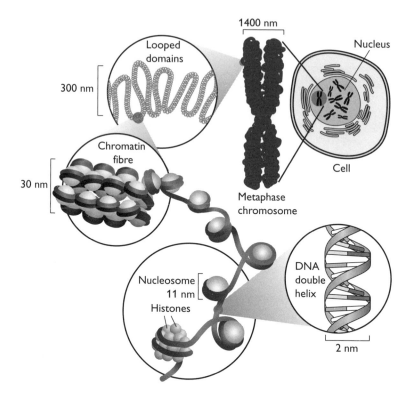

Figure 8 The organisation of DNA into chromosomes in a eukaryotic cell

The association of eukaryotic DNA with histones helps to compact the molecule into a smaller space and to protect the DNA, further improving its stability.

How DNA directs the cell to produce proteins

Each protein is made from one or more polypeptide chains. A polypeptide contains many amino acids linked together by peptide bonds. The nature and sequence of the amino acids in a polypeptide chain is determined by the nature and sequence of the bases in the gene that directs the synthesis of that polypeptide. Each triplet of bases codes for one amino acid.

- The DNA code is 'rewritten' in a molecule of **messenger RNA (mRNA)** that travels from the nucleus through pores in the nuclear envelope to the ribosomes. This rewriting of the code is called **transcription**.
- Free amino acids are transferred from the cytoplasm to the ribosomes. This is carried out by molecules of **transfer RNA (tRNA)**.
- The RNA code is 'read' and the amino acids are assembled into a polypeptide. This is called **translation** and is carried out by the ribosomes. This will later be folded to give the tertiary structure of the protein.

First position		Second position				Third position
	T	C	A	G	
T	Phenylalanine	Serine	Tyrosine	Cysteine	T
	Phenylalanine	Serine	Tyrosine	Cysteine	C
	Leucine	Serine	stop	stop	A
	Leucine	Serine	stop	Tryptophan	G
C	Leucine	Proline	Histidine	Arginine	T
	Leucine	Proline	Histidine	Arginine	C
	Leucine	Proline	Glutamine	Arginine	A
	Leucine	Proline	Glutamine	Arginine	G
A	Isoleucine	Threonine	Asparagine	Serine	T
	Isoleucine	Threonine	Asparagine	Serine	C
	Isoleucine	Threonine	Lysine	Arginine	A
	Methionine	Threonine	Lysine	Arginine	G
G	Valine	Alanine	Aspartic acid	Glycine	T
	Valine	Alanine	Aspartic acid	Glycine	C
	Valine	Alanine	Glutamic acid	Glycine	A
	Valine	Alanine	Glutamic acid	Glycine	G

Figure 9 The genetic code

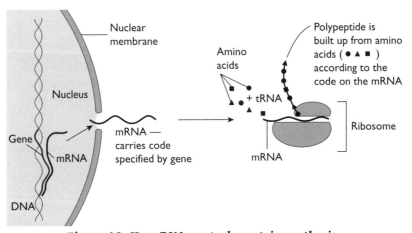

Figure 10 How DNA controls protein synthesis

Mutations

A mutation is a change in the base sequence of a DNA molecule. There are many different kinds of mutation, but even the smallest can have a significant effect. Point mutations affect just one base in the DNA molecule. However, even this may result in a change in the protein produced, as it changes the triplet that codes for one of the amino acids.

Original code	TTA	CGG	ATC	TCC
Amino acids	Leucine	Arginine	Isoleucine	Serine

Changed code	TTC	CGG	ATC	TCC
Amino acids	Phenylalanine	Arginine	Isoleucine	Serine
	CHANGED SEQUENCE			

Figure 11 A change in base sequence may result in a new amino acid

A new amino acid will result in a different polypeptide being synthesised. This could result in either:

- a different structural protein, for example a different haemoglobin, such as that which causes sickle-cell anaemia, or
- a non-functional enzyme, which could result in a metabolic pathway being interrupted

However, because the genetic code is degenerate, a point mutation need not result in a new amino acid.

Original code	TTA	CGG	ATC	TCC
Amino acids	Leucine	Arginine	Isoleucine	Serine

Changed code	TTA	CGG	ATC	TCG
Amino acids	Leucine	Arginine	Isoleucine	Serine
	NO CHANGE TO SEQUENCE			

Figure 12 The degenerate nature of the genetic code means changes in base sequence do not always cause changes in amino acid sequence

Non-coding DNA

There are sequences of bases within a gene called **introns** that do not code for any of the amino acids in the final polypeptide chain. The coding regions are called **exons**. When the DNA is transcribed to mRNA, the introns are enzymically 'cut out' of the transcribed mRNA.

There are also base sequences between genes that do not code for amino acids. They often contain repeating trinucleotides containing cystosine and guanine, for example CAG or CGG. These sections are called minisatellites or microsatellites (which are smaller with fewer repeats).

There are a great number of these microsatellites and minisatellites in the human genome and each is extremely variable between individuals. The variability of minisatellite DNA and microsatellite DNA is the basis of genetic fingerprinting. It is extremely unlikely that two individuals will have the same versions of several minisatellites or microsatellites.

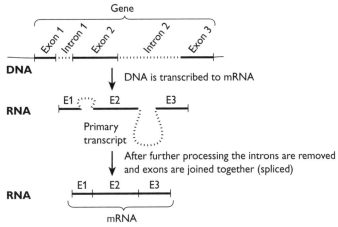

In a gene there are non-coding sections of DNA called introns, separating the coding regions or exons. Introns are transcribed but are later 'cut out' of the final mRNA molecule.

Figure 13 Introns and exons

What the examiners could ask you to do

- Explain any of the key concepts.
- Recall and show understanding of any of the key facts.
- Label a diagram of a DNA molecule.
- Use the genetic code to predict the amino acid content of a polypeptide, given the base sequence of a section of DNA.
- Use the genetic code to predict whether a change in the DNA sequence will produce a change in the final polypeptide or not.
- Compare and contrast the DNA in prokaryotic cells and eukaryotic cells.

Passing on the genetic material

Key concepts you must understand

DNA must be passed on to:
- the next generation of cells (**daughter cells**), when cells in the body divide to bring about growth or repair
- the next generation of individuals

To pass on DNA to the daughter cells, the DNA in the **parent cells** must **replicate** itself faithfully so that the daughter cells are genetically identical to each other and to the parent cell.

In most cases, it is advantageous for the next generation of individuals *not* to be genetically identical, but to show genetic variation. This gives the species as a whole a better chance of survival if the environment changes.

To achieve genetic variation in the next generation of individuals, the **gametes** (sex cells) that will fuse to start the next generation must vary.

Gametes must also have only half the amount of DNA (and so, half the number of chromosomes) of the parent cell, so that when two of them fuse, the full amount is restored.

The full number of chromosomes is the **diploid number** and the number present in gametes is the **haploid number**.

The chromosomes in human cells exist in pairs called **homologous chromosomes**. By the time the cell enters cell division, each chromosome has been duplicated to form a pair of **sister chromatids**.

Each pair of chromosomes carries genes for the same feature in the same sequence, but the alleles of the genes may be different. The alleles on the sister chromatids of one chromosome are identical.

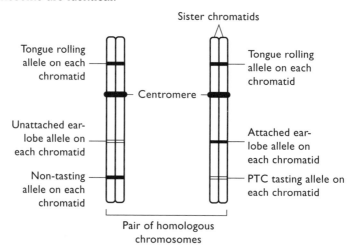

Figure 14 Homologous chromosomes

To produce diploid genetically identical daughter cells, the parent cells divide by **mitosis**. To produce haploid, genetically varying gametes, cells divide by **meiosis**.

Cell division by mitosis normally takes place in a very controlled way. It is regulated by a number of genes. However, sometimes these controls fail and mitosis takes place in an uncontrolled manner. This leads to the formation of a **tumour**.

Tumours can be **benign** or **malignant**. Benign tumours are usually slow-growing and do not spread to other parts of the body. Malignant tumours grow much more quickly and often spread. It is these tumours that form **cancers**.

Key facts you must know and understand

DNA replication

DNA molecules exist within chromosomes in the nucleus and are surrounded by a 'soup' of free DNA nucleotides. These nucleotides are used to build new strands of DNA. The process involves several enzymes and proteins, but the key stages are as follows:

- Molecules of the enzyme **DNA helicase** break hydrogen bonds holding the two polynucleotide strands together and 'unwind' part of the DNA molecule, revealing two single-stranded regions.
- Molecules of **DNA polymerase** follow the helicase along each single-stranded region, which acts as a template for the synthesis of a new strand.
- The DNA polymerase assembles free DNA nucleotides into a new strand alongside each of the template strands. The base sequence in each of these new strands is complementary to its template strand because of the base-pairing rule — A-T, C-G (see page 16).
- The processes of unwinding followed by complementary strand synthesis progress along the whole length of the DNA molecule.

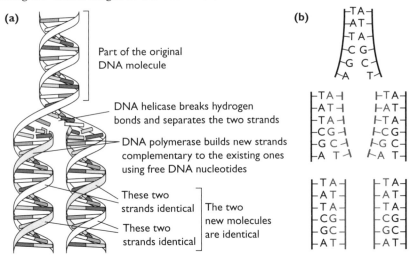

Figure 15 (a) DNA replication; (b) semi-conservative replication of DNA

This method of replicating DNA is called **semi-conservative replication**. It ensures that:

- each new DNA molecule formed contains one strand from the original DNA (and one newly synthesised strand)
- both new DNA molecules formed are identical to each other and to the original molecule

The cell cycle

Cells are lost from the surface of the skin each time we touch something. These cells are replaced from a layer of cells below the skin's surface that divide repeatedly by mitosis. However, that layer must also maintain *itself*, for if it were lost, we would lose the ability to replace lost skin cells. Figure 16 shows how this is achieved.

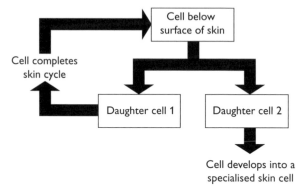

Figure 16 Skin cell cycle

Cells that divide repeatedly to replace those lost, such as cells in the skin or stem cells in bone marrow, go through a cycle of events called the **cell cycle**. These events ultimately allow the cell to divide to form two cells by mitotic division. One of these cells eventually becomes a specialised cell (like a skin cell); the other completes the cell cycle and replaces the original cell, so that the process can be repeated.

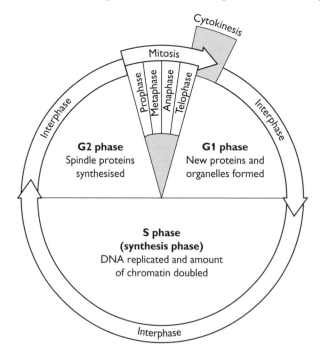

Figure 17 The cell cycle

A cell that has just been produced by cell division must go through the following stages if it is to divide again:

- It must grow. Initially, the cell is half the size of the parent cell, with only half the organelles of a full-sized cell. During this phase of the cell cycle, more organelles are synthesised and the cell enlarges. Nucleotides and histone proteins are synthesised in preparation for DNA replication later in the cycle. This is the **G1 phase** of the cell cycle.
- DNA must replicate itself and combine with newly synthesised histone proteins to double the amount of chromatin in the nucleus. The cell continues to grow. This is the **S phase** of the cell cycle.
- The cell must prepare itself for mitosis. Specialised proteins called tubulins are synthesised. These are used to make the spindle apparatus, which will eventually separate the chromosomes. This is the **G2 phase** of the cell cycle.
- The G1, S and G2 phases are collectively known as **interphase**.
- The nucleus of the cell now divides by mitosis. Once mitosis is complete, the cell divides into two cells during **cytokinesis**.

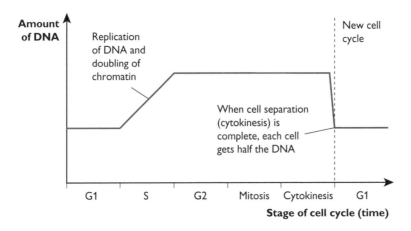

Figure 18 The changes in DNA content during the cell cycle

Mitosis

Mitotic cell division involves a division of the nucleus followed by the cell dividing and producing two cells. Strictly, mitosis refers only to division of the nucleus.

Mitosis results in two cells with the same number and type of chromosomes as each other and as the parent cell that formed them. They are genetically identical.

The process is divided into four key stages: **prophase**, **metaphase**, **anaphase** and **telophase**.

> **Tip** You do not need to know anything at all about the subdivisions of prophase.

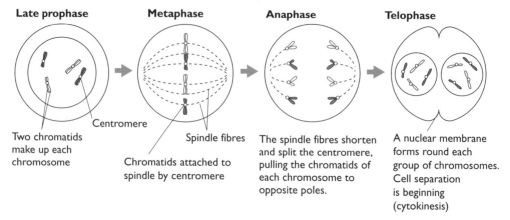

Late prophase **Metaphase** **Anaphase** **Telophase**

Centromere

Two chromatids make up each chromosome

Spindle fibres

Chromatids attached to spindle by centromere

The spindle fibres shorten and split the centromere, pulling the chromatids of each chromosome to opposite poles.

A nuclear membrane forms round each group of chromosomes. Cell separation is beginning (cytokinesis)

Figure 19 Stages of mitosis

Stage of mitosis	Main events
Prophase	Chromosomes coil and become visible as double structures. Each is called a chromatid. (During interphase, the DNA replicated and from one chromosome two identical **sister chromatids** were formed.) They are held together by a **centromere**. The nuclear envelope starts to break down.
Metaphase	The spindle forms. The centromeres attach the chromatids to the spindle fibres so that they lie across the middle of the spindle.
Anaphase	The spindle fibres shorten and pull the sister chromatids to opposite poles of the cell. Once the chromatids have been separated, they are called chromosomes again.
Telophase	The spindle fibres are broken down. The two sets of chromosomes group together at each pole and a nuclear envelope forms around each. The chromosomes uncoil and cannot be seen as individual structures.

Tip You may be given a series of diagrams of the stages of mitosis and asked to place them in the correct sequence. Make sure you know the main features of each stage.

Meiosis

Meiotic cell division also involves division of the nucleus (**meiosis**) and division of the cell (**cytokinesis**). However, in each full meiotic division, this happens twice to produce four daughter cells.

- Meiosis I — this separates the chromosomes from each homologous pair into different cells, halving the chromosome number.
- Meiosis II — this separates the chromatids in each chromosome, rather like mitosis.

Tip Be quite clear in your mind that the *chromosome* number is halved after the first meiotic division; the cells formed at this stage are haploid cells.

The main stages of meiosis I

These are outlined in Figure 20 (a).

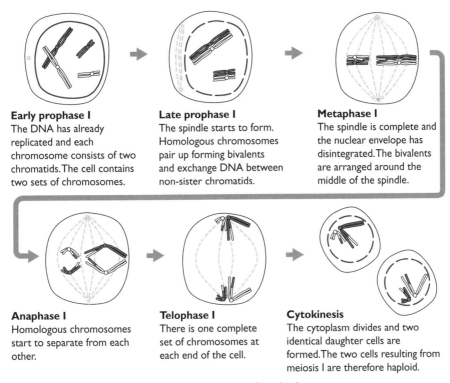

Early prophase I
The DNA has already replicated and each chromosome consists of two chromatids. The cell contains two sets of chromosomes.

Late prophase I
The spindle starts to form. Homologous chromosomes pair up forming bivalents and exchange DNA between non-sister chromatids.

Metaphase I
The spindle is complete and the nuclear envelope has disintegrated. The bivalents are arranged around the middle of the spindle.

Anaphase I
Homologous chromosomes start to separate from each other.

Telophase I
There is one complete set of chromosomes at each end of the cell.

Cytokinesis
The cytoplasm divides and two identical daughter cells are formed. The two cells resulting from meiosis I are therefore haploid.

Figure 20 (a) Stages of meiosis I

Crossing over

Crossing over is a 'cut-and-paste' event that occurs when the two homologous chromosomes form a bivalent.

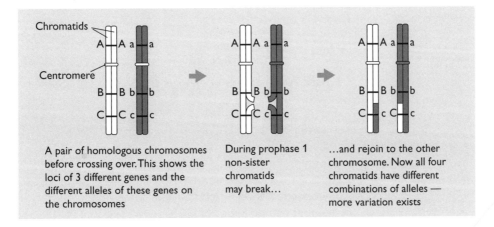

A pair of homologous chromosomes before crossing over. This shows the loci of 3 different genes and the different alleles of these genes on the chromosomes

During prophase 1 non-sister chromatids may break...

...and rejoin to the other chromosome. Now all four chromatids have different combinations of alleles — more variation exists

Random segregation

The way in which the bivalents are aligned at metaphase determines how they will be segregated into the two new cells.

Sometimes the chromosomes line up like this... ...giving this outcome

...and sometimes like this ...giving a different outcome

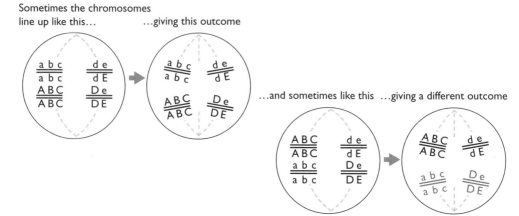

The main stages of meiosis II

These are outlined in Figure 20 (b)

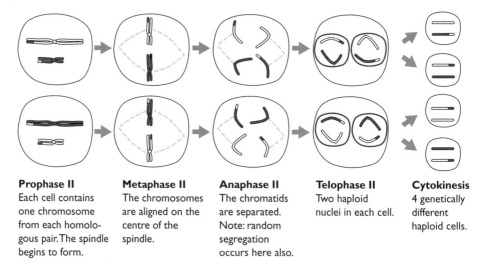

Prophase II	**Metaphase II**	**Anaphase II**	**Telophase II**	**Cytokinesis**
Each cell contains one chromosome from each homologous pair. The spindle begins to form.	The chromosomes are aligned on the centre of the spindle.	The chromatids are separated. Note: random segregation occurs here also.	Two haploid nuclei in each cell.	4 genetically different haploid cells.

Figure 20 (b) Stages of meiosis II

Meiotic cell division

The key features of a meiotic cell division are that:

- it involves two nuclear divisions
- four daughter cells are formed
- the cells formed are haploid
- the daughter cells show genetic variation (contain the same number and type of chromosomes, but different combinations of alleles)

Meiosis and mitosis compared

Feature of the process	Mitosis	Meiosis
Number of nuclear divisions	One	Two
Number of daughter cells formed	Two	Four
Chromosome number of daughter cells	Diploid	Haploid
Genetic variation in daughter cells	No	Yes
Appearance of chromosomes at anaphase	Single structures	Anaphase I — double structures Anaphase II — single structures
Number of chromosomes moving to each pole at anaphase	Diploid number	Haploid number (both I and II)

> **Tip** The number and appearance of the chromosomes at anaphase can be used to identify a cell division as mitotic or meiotic. If the chromosomes are double structures (two chromatids) it can only be anaphase I of meiosis. If the chromosomes are single structures, it could be mitosis or anaphase II of meiosis. In that case, look at how many there are. If the diploid number is moving to each pole, it must be mitosis; if the haploid number is moving to each pole, it must be meiosis (II).

The cell cycle and the formation of tumours

Tumours form when a cell divides by mitosis in an uncontrolled fashion. Most tumours are benign. These are usually slow growing and often harmless, although they may cause problems because of *where* they grow. A benign tumour in the brain may exert pressure on a region of the brain. Malignant tumours divide more quickly, in a more uncontrolled way and are much more dangerous. It is these that we call cancers.

Benign tumours and malignant tumours differ in a number of important ways:
- Benign tumours usually grow much more slowly than malignant tumours.
- Benign tumours usually remain encased within a fibrous capsule and do not invade the tissue in which they originated. The boundaries of malignant tumours are much less defined and the cells frequently invade the tissue in which they originate.
- Benign tumours rarely show **metastasis** (spread to other parts of the body). Many malignant tumours do **metastasise** and cause **secondary cancers.**

There are a number of control mechanisms that normally operate to prevent cell division from going out of control and forming tumours. **Proto-oncogenes** are inactive genes that are present in all our cells. They can be transformed into active **oncogenes** in a number of ways. The gene may mutate, or it may be influenced by a viral infection.

Active oncogenes interfere with the normal regulation of cellular metabolism. The result is loss of control over cell division. In effect, a switch is set that says 'keep dividing'.

However, DNA that is damaged by mutation is often repaired by the action of proteins produced by other genes. Therefore, for a tumour to develop, this mechanism must fail too.

A third set of genes (**tumour-suppressor genes**) is also involved. These genes become active when a group of cells is dividing in an uncontrolled manner. They 'switch off' the division process. For a tumour to keep on developing, these genes must also fail.

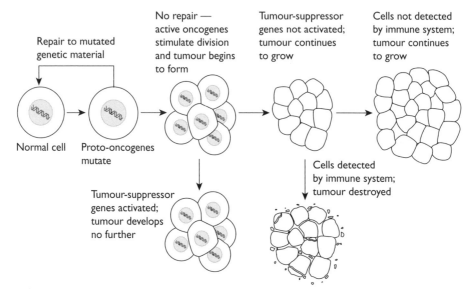

Figure 21 Stages in the development of a tumour

Tip You may be asked to interpret data relating to the effect of environmental factors on the incidence or rate of growth of tumours. Remember, some of the evidence is correlational and some is experimental, with cause and effect isolated and other variables controlled. Make sure you can distinguish between the two and that your answer does not go beyond the evidence.

What the examiners could ask you to do

- Explain any of the key concepts.
- Recall and show understanding of any of the key facts.
- Put diagrams showing the stages of mitosis into sequence.
- Identify a drawing of a stage of cell division and say whether it is mitosis or meiosis.
- Interpret graphs showing changes in the DNA content of a cell at different stages of the cell cycle.
- Identify from drawings or data whether a tumour is benign or malignant.
- Interpret data relating to the influence of environmental factors on the growth of tumours.
- Use your knowledge of the cell cycle to deduce how cancer treatments may work.

The genetic diversity of populations

Key concepts you must understand

Mutations create new genes. Crossing over and random segregation of chromosomes during meiosis, together with random fertilisation of gametes during sexual reproduction, create new combinations of alleles.

Random fertilisation results in even more genetic diversity if mating is also random. This type of mating is called **out-breeding**.

The **founder effect**, **genetic bottlenecks**, **in-breeding** and **selective breeding** tend to reduce genetic diversity.

Key facts you must know and understand

The founder effect

In the founder effect, a few individuals colonise a new environment (the colonisers carry the population forwards in space).

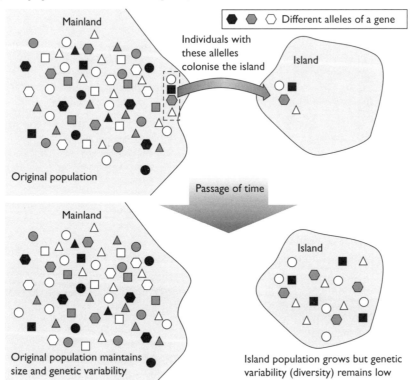

Figure 22 Consequences of the founder effect

Only a fraction of the alleles that were present in the original population is present in the small section that colonises the new environment to establish a new population. Therefore, the genetic diversity of the new population will be reduced.

Examples of the founder effect include:
- the Afrikaner population of South Africa, which is descended from just a few Dutch settlers
- the grey squirrel population in the UK, which is descended from a small number of colonising individuals

Genetic bottlenecks

In a genetic bottleneck, the population is reduced drastically by some environmental effect such as a disease (the surviving members carry the population forwards in time). Only a fraction of the alleles that were present in the original population is present in the small number of survivors that carries the population forward. Therefore, the genetic diversity of the new population will be reduced.

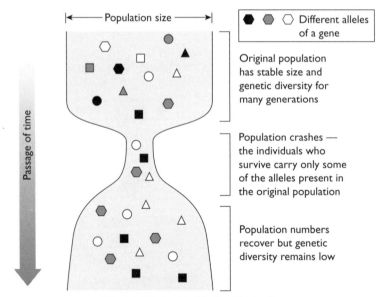

Figure 23 A genetic bottleneck

Examples of genetic bottlenecks include:
- the population of lions in Tanzania, which crashed from 75 individuals in 1962 to just 7 in 1964
- the cheetah population in Africa, which crashed dramatically about 10000 years ago

The population size may recover after a bottleneck event, but if the population crash is too great, it may lead to extinction.

Genetic diversity remains low after a founder effect or a genetic bottleneck because mating, although possibly random, is not true **out-breeding**. It is restricted to mating between the few genetic types that survive in the new population and is effectively an example of **in-breeding**, where mating is restricted to just a few types. In-breeding maintains a low genetic diversity.

Conservation projects designed to maintain and increase populations of threatened species (such as the cheetah populations) often encourage breeding between animals from different populations. This is a kind of forced out-breeding designed to maximise genetic diversity in each population by introducing alleles from other populations.

Selective breeding

Selective breeding is a form of in-breeding that is controlled by humans. For thousands of years, genetic modification for increased yields was achieved by careful breeding of selected strains of stock animals and crop plants. This meant only allowing breeding between high-yielding plants or animals, with the result that many of the alleles in the original gene pool were excluded from subsequent generations. They were only passed on if, by chance, they were found in an organism that had desirable alleles for, say, increased milk yield.

Examples of selective breeding include:
- cattle bred for either meat or milk yield
- pigs, descended from wild boars and bred to produce large litters (between 12 and 20 piglets) that grow quickly
- modern wheat, descended from grasses and selectively bred to give a high grain yield and be resistant to diseases

> **Tip** You may be given information concerning the selective breeding of stock animals and asked to comment on the ethics of the process. You must not give an emotional response. It should be a balanced response that presents advantages and disadvantages.

Processes that increase genetic diversity include:
- mutation
- crossing over
- random segregation of chromosomes
- random fertilisation
- out-breeding

Processes that decrease genetic diversity include:
- the founder effect
- genetic bottlenecks
- in-breeding
- selective breeding

What the examiners could ask you to do

- Explain any of the key concepts.
- Recall and show understanding of any of the key facts.
- Interpret data showing changes in genetic diversity in terms of genetic bottlenecks, founder effects, selective breeding, in-breeding and out-breeding.
- Explain the theory behind breeding programmes of threatened species.
- Interpret data on selective breeding, giving advantages and disadvantages, and commenting on the ethics of the process.

Selection in a population

Key concepts you must understand

Charles Darwin first developed the idea of **natural selection**. As a result of his observations he concluded that:

- all species tend to produce more offspring than can possibly survive
- there is variation among the offspring

From these observations he deduced that:

- there will be a 'struggle for existence' between members of a species, because they over-reproduce, and resources are limited
- because of variation, some members of a species will be better adapted than others to their environment

Combining these two deductions, Darwin proposed:

'Those members of a species which are best adapted to their environment will survive and reproduce in greater numbers than others less well adapted.'

This was his now famous theory of natural selection.

Darwin knew little of genetics. However, we can modify his theory to take account of gene action. Genes or, more precisely, alleles of genes, determine features. Suppose an allele determines a feature that gives an organism an advantage in its environment. As the individuals with the advantage survive and reproduce in greater numbers, the frequency of the advantageous allele in the population will increase.

Mutations introduce new alleles into populations. Any mutation could:

- confer a selective advantage — the frequency of the allele will increase over time
- be neutral in its overall effect — the frequency may increase slowly, remain stable or decrease (the change in frequency will depend on what other genes/alleles are associated with the mutation)
- be disadvantageous — the frequency of the allele will be low and the allele could disappear from the population

> **Tip** You may be presented with data concerning an unfamiliar example of natural selection. To help you to answer such questions, you should consider:
> - What factor creates the selection pressure?
> - What is the variation that exists?
> - Which of the variants will be at an advantage and why?
> - What will be the consequences for the various types and allele frequencies?
> Explain these in terms of survival, reproduction and passing on alleles to the next generation.

Key facts you must know and understand

The effects of antibiotics on bacterial populations

Antibiotics act against bacteria by disrupting cellular processes such as:

- DNA replication
- protein synthesis
- cell wall synthesis

Some antibiotics kill bacteria — these are **bactericidal** antibiotics. Others do not kill bacteria but stop them from reproducing — these are **bacteriostatic** antibiotics.

The ways in which some different antibiotics act are summarised in the table below.

Mode of action of antibiotic	Example	How the antibiotic works	Bactericidal or bacteriostatic?
Disrupts cell wall synthesis	Penicillin	Weakened cell wall cannot resist entry of water by osmosis and cell bursts (osmotic lysis)	Bactericidal
Disrupts DNA replication	Nalidixic acid	Bacteria are not killed, but cell division is halted	Bacteriostatic
Disrupts protein synthesis	Tetracycline	Bacterial cell cannot synthesise enzymes and structural proteins	Bactericidal

Antibiotics that disrupt cell wall synthesis interfere with the synthesis of the peptido-glycan layer in the cell wall. Water enters by osmosis down a water potential gradient. Ordinarily, this entry would be resisted by the cell wall. With only an incomplete cell wall to resist the swelling caused by the entry of water, the bacterial cell bursts.

How the repeated use of antibiotics changes bacterial populations

Bacterial cells contain two types of DNA. Most bacterial DNA is organised into a single large, cyclical molecule, but some bacterial DNA is found as **plasmids**. These are small, circular molecules of DNA, separate from the main DNA.

Mutations in the plasmid DNA can produce resistance to an antibiotic. Bacteria can pass on these mutations in two ways. The obvious way is that when they reproduce, the offspring will inherit the mutation.

Bacterial cell about to divide by binary fission   Bacterial cells formed from division

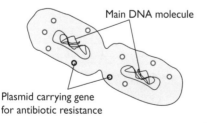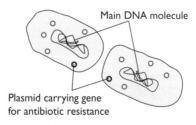

Main DNA molecule   Main DNA molecule

Plasmid carrying gene for antibiotic resistance   Plasmid carrying gene for antibiotic resistance

Both 'daughter' bacteria are resistant to the antibiotic

Figure 24 The gene for antibiotic resistance is passed on when bacteria reproduce by binary fission

Bacteria reproduce by a process called **binary fission**. All the DNA in the bacterium replicates prior to reproduction, not just the main DNA molecule. When the bacterial cell divides, each daughter cell will receive some plasmids that carry the gene for resistance to the antibiotic. This is sometimes referred to as **vertical transmission**.

However, they can also pass plasmids to other bacteria that happen to be around — as well as receive plasmids from these bacteria. The process is a kind of genetic swap-shop called **conjugation**. Plasmids pass through **conjugation tubes** from one bacterium to another. This is sometimes referred to as **horizontal transmission**.

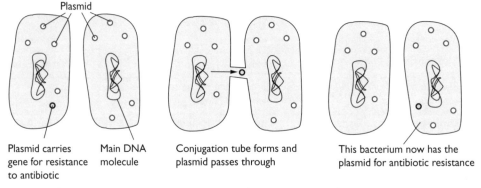

Plasmid

Plasmid carries gene for resistance to antibiotic

Main DNA molecule

Conjugation tube forms and plasmid passes through

This bacterium now has the plasmid for antibiotic resistance

Figure 25 How plasmids can pass from one bacterium to another

It is possible that conjugation is the main mechanism by which some bacteria have become resistant to *several* antibiotics — multiple antibody resistance.

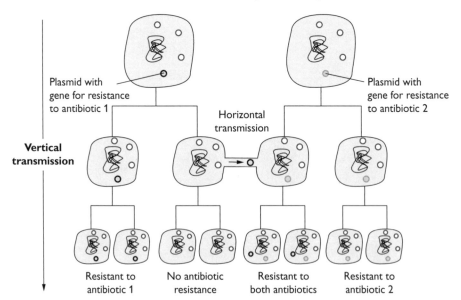

Plasmid with gene for resistance to antibiotic 1

Plasmid with gene for resistance to antibiotic 2

Horizontal transmission

Vertical transmission

Resistant to antibiotic 1

No antibiotic resistance

Resistant to both antibiotics

Resistant to antibiotic 2

Figure 26 The importance of vertical and horizontal transmission in passing on antibiotic resistance in bacteria

A mutation conferring resistance only gives a selective advantage if the antibiotic is being used. In this case, it creates a **selection pressure** in favour of those bacteria that have the resistance and against those that do not have it.

More of the bacteria with the resistance survive to reproduce than those without the resistance. The frequency of the allele for resistance increases and will increase with each succeeding generation of bacteria, until nearly all the population carries the resistant allele. This is summarised in the table below.

Selection pressure	Repeated use of an antibiotic
Variation in the population	Chance mutations in some individuals confer resistance
Which are at an advantage?	Resistant forms
Consequences for phenotype	Resistant forms survive and reproduce in greater numbers — with time, more of the population are resistant
Consequences for allele frequencies	Alleles conferring resistance are passed on in increasing numbers with each generation — frequency increases

What the examiners could ask you to do

- Explain any of the key concepts.
- Recall and show understanding of any of the key facts.
- Interpret data concerning selection in a novel situation.
- Comment on the procedures used in investigations of selection in microorganisms and other organisms.
- Comment on the significance to society of multiple resistance in bacteria, with particular reference to healthcare.

Different sized organisms

Key concepts you must understand

As organisms have evolved, there has been a general increase in size. This has had big implications for gas exchange and transport.

The total surface area of an exchange surface determines the maximum potential rate of obtaining oxygen. This is also influenced by:
- difference in concentration across the exchange surface (the diffusion gradient)
- the thickness of the exchange surface (the length of the diffusion pathway)

The total volume of an organism determines the maximum rate at which the oxygen can be used. This is also influenced by:
- metabolic rate (the rate at which energy-consuming processes are happening)
- activity and temperature (which influence metabolic rate)

The ratio between surface area and volume is a crude measure of the ratio of supply of oxygen to the demand for oxygen.

If the organism is a cube and the length of each edge is 1 arbitrary unit (au), then:
- the area of each face is $1 \times 1 = 1\ au^2$
- there are six faces to a cube, so the total surface area is $6\ au^2$
- the volume is $1 \times 1 \times 1 = 1\ au^3$
- the ratio of surface area to volume $= 6/1 = 6$

In a bigger organism, where the length of each edge is 2 au:
- the area of each face is $2 \times 2 = 4\ au^2$
- there are six faces to a cube, so the total surface area is $24\ au^2$
- the volume is $2 \times 2 \times 2 = 8\ au^3$
- the ratio of surface area to volume $= 24/8 = 3$

If you calculate the values for cubes of edge 4 au and 8 au, you will find that the surface area-to-volume ratios are 1.5 and 0.75 respectively.

Figure 27 illustrates the effect of increasing body size on surface area to volume ratio.

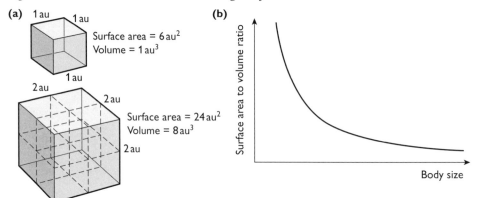

Figure 27 (a) The effect of increasing size on the surface area and volume of a cube (b) As organisms became larger through evolution, the ratio of surface area to volume became smaller

Very small organisms obtain oxygen by simple diffusion through their surface. The demand for oxygen is satisfied by the rate at which it can be supplied.

In bigger organisms, one of two strategies was adopted during evolution:
- They evolved body shapes that retained a large surface area to volume ratio, such as cylinders (worms) or flat, thin bodies (flatworms). Cylindrical and thin, flat bodies impose a limit on body size as a narrow cylinder or a thin, flat body can only support a certain body mass.
- They evolved specialised gas exchange organs with a huge surface area; this restored the surface area-to-volume ratio needed to supply sufficient oxygen.

The evolution of specialised gas exchange organs meant that a transport system had to evolve at the same time in order to distribute the oxygen around the body.

In mammals and fish, the concentration difference (diffusion gradient) of oxygen across a gas exchange surface is maintained by:
- blood flow — this carries oxygenated blood away from the exchange surface and replaces it with deoxygenated blood — keeping the concentration low on this side of the exchange surface
- ventilation — this continually replaces the oxygen-containing medium (air or water) — keeping the concentration high on this side of the exchange surface

A reverse logic applies for CO_2.

Diffusion over long distances is a slow and inefficient process, as the concentration difference between adjacent points along the pathway is very small. To make exchange efficient, mass flow systems move a medium containing the substance to be exchanged to and from the exchange surface, where diffusion can then occur efficiently. Examples of mass flow systems include:
- systems that move an oxygen-containing medium to and from a gas exchange surface
- transport systems

In mammals, exchange between blood and cells occurs through **tissue fluid** lost from the blood.

Key facts you must know and understand

Gas exchange surfaces in different organisms
Unicellular protoctistans
Unicellular protoctistans, such as *Amoeba*, exchange gases through the plasma membrane of their single cell (which is also their body surface). The large surface area-to-volume ratio means that demand for oxygen is unlikely to outstrip supply.

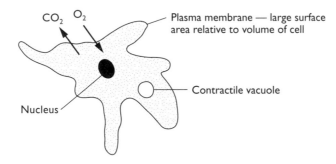

Figure 28 Gas exchange in Amoeba (a unicellular protoctist)

Fish
Fish have **gills** that extract oxygen dissolved in water.

Each gill is divided into many **gill filaments** attached to a bony gill arch. This increases the total surface area of the gill.

Each gill filament has many **gill lamellae**, which increase the surface area still further. These lamellae have very thin walls to shorten the diffusion pathway.

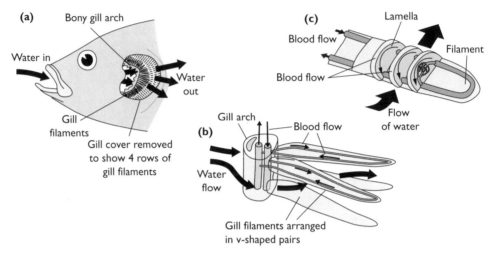

Figure 32 The structure of (a) gills and (b) gill filaments; (c) blood flow in lamellae

Notice that as water flows past the lamellae, it flows in the opposite direction to the blood in the lamellae. This **counter current** maintains a concentration gradient for both carbon dioxide and oxygen between the water and the blood, and improves the efficiency of gas exchange.

Insects

Insects do not have lungs or gills, but a **tracheal system** that consists of two main **tracheae** running the length of the insect's body. Each trachea opens to the air through several **spiracles** along its length.

Smaller tubes, **tracheoles**, branch off the tracheae and carry air directly to the cells of the insect's body. The large numbers of tracheoles create a large gas exchange surface and the thin wall of the smallest of these ensures a short diffusion distance.

The air sacs function as a temporary store. To minimise water loss by evaporation in hot conditions, insects close the spiracles and use oxygen from air stored in the sacs.

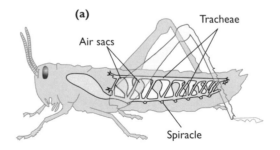

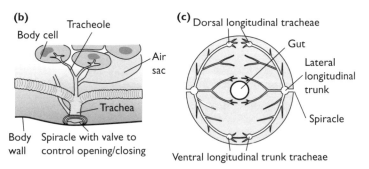

Figure 30 (a) The tracheal system of an insect (b) The relationship between spiracles, trachea and tracheoles (c) Diagrammatic representation of the insect tracheal system

In larger insects there is some ventilation of the system, resulting in mass flow. By opening some spiracles and closing others whilst dilating and constricting the abdomen, air (*not* oxygen or carbon dioxide) can be moved along the trachea. However, individual gases, rather than air, still *diffuse* to and from cells along the tracheoles.

The spongy mesophyll of a leaf

Because they are loosely packed, the surface area of spongy mesophyll cells in contact with the air spaces is large enough to allow effective diffusion of gases. The air spaces also create a free diffusion pathway from stomata to the palisade cells at the top of the leaf.

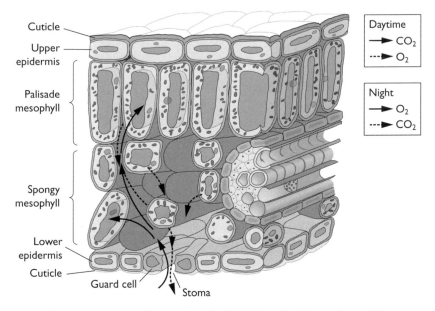

Figure 31 Gas exchange in a leaf during the day and at night

The principal features of these four exchange surfaces are compared in the table below.

Feature of gas exchange surface	Surface of protoctistan	Fish gill lamellae	Insect tracheoles	Spongy mesophyll
Respiratory medium	Water	Water	Air	Air
Exchange surface	Plasma membrane	Gill lamellae	Tracheoles	Plasma membranes of spongy mesophyll cells
Ventilation	None	Movements of mouth and gill cover create one-way flow	Abdomen dilates/contracts decreasing/ increasing pressure	None
Large surface area-to-volume ratio due to:	Small volume of cell	Large area of lamellae	Large area of tracheoles	Large area of cell surfaces and loose packing of cells
Concentration gradient maintained by:	Use of oxygen in cell	Ventilation/ counter-current system in lamellae	Ventilation/use of oxygen in body cells	Use of oxygen by mesophyll cells
Exchange surface thin due to:	Thin plasma membrane	Thin walls of lamellae	Thin walls of tracheoles	Only cell wall and membrane at exchange surface

Transport systems in different organisms
Mammals

Blood is moved through a system of blood vessels by the pumping of the heart. Mammals have a double circulation, in which blood passes through the heart twice in a complete circulation of the body. The diagram below shows the main components of this system.

There are three main types of blood vessel:
- **Arteries** carry blood under high pressure away from the heart to the organs (**arterioles** are small arteries).
- **Veins** carry blood under low pressure away from the organs towards the heart (**venules** are small veins).
- **Capillaries** carry blood close to every cell within an organ.

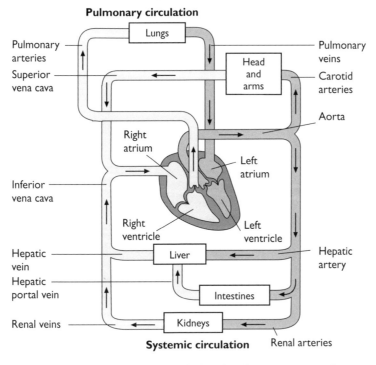

Figure 32 The main components of the circulatory system of a mammal

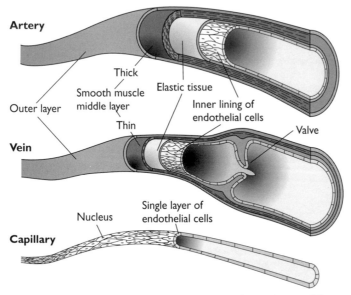

Figure 33 Structure of an artery, a vein and a capillary

The adaptations of the structure of each type of blood vessel to its main function are shown in the table below.

Feature	Artery	Arteriole	Capillary	Vein
Cross-section of vessel	⊚	⊚	○	◎
Structural features	Thick wall and small lumen	Thinner wall than artery with relatively more muscle	Microscopic vessels, wall only one cell thick	Thin wall, little muscle, large lumen, valves
Blood flow	Away from heart, towards an organ	Within an organ, to capillaries in different parts of the organ	Around cells of an organ	Away from an organ towards the heart
Type of blood	Oxygenated*	Oxygenated*	Oxygenated * blood becomes deoxygenated	Deoxygenated*
Blood pressure	High and in pulses (pulsatile)	Lower than arteries and less pulsatile	Pressure falls throughout capillary network	Low and non-pulsatile
Main functions of vessels	Transport of blood to organs	Transport of blood within an organ; redistribution of blood flow	Formation of tissue fluid to allow exchange between blood and cells of an organ	Transport of blood back to the heart
Adaptations to main function	Large amount of elastic tissue allows stretching due to surges in pressure and recoil afterwards; endothelium provides smooth inner surface to reduce resistance	Large amount of smooth muscle under nervous control allows redistribution of blood; constriction limits blood flow, dilation increases blood flow	Small size allows close contact with all cells in the body; thin, permeable (leaky) walls allow formation of tissue fluid for exchange	Large lumen and thin wall offer least resistance to blood flow as blood is under low pressure; valves prevent backflow of blood

* reversed in pulmonary and umbilical arteries and veins

The formation of tissue fluid and exchange between blood and cells
Blood flows close to every cell of the body in the capillary networks, in all organs. However, it is tissue fluid, not blood, which carries glucose and oxygen to the cells as well as carbon dioxide and other waste products in the opposite direction. Tissue fluid is formed from blood in every capillary network.

Tissue fluid flows around the cells, bathing them in a fluid that provides a constant environment. The constant pH and temperature of the tissue fluid help to provide optimum conditions for enzyme activity in the cells.

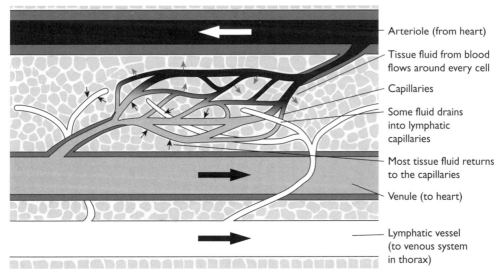

Figure 34 The circulation of tissue fluid and the formation of lymph

Tissue fluid forms because the capillary walls are permeable to most molecules. However, **plasma protein** molecules are too large to escape and so are not found in tissue fluid.

Two forces influence the formation and reabsorption of tissue fluid:
- the hydrostatic pressure of the blood (due to the pumping of the heart), which tends to force liquid out of the capillaries
- the difference in water potentials between the plasma and the surrounding tissue fluid, which could act either way, depending on the balance

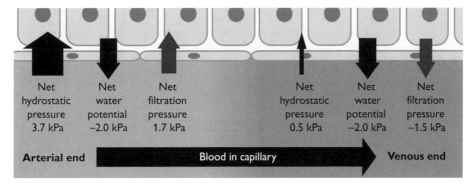

Figure 35 The forces involved in the formation and reabsorption of tissue fluid

At the arterial end of a capillary network:
- the hydrostatic effect is greater than that of the water potential difference
- there is a net outward pressure
- tissue fluid (all the substances in the plasma except proteins) is forced out of the capillaries

The loss of fluid reduces the hydrostatic pressure of the blood, while the water potential remains more or less unchanged.

At the venous end of the capillary network:
- the effect of the water potential difference is greater than that of the hydrostatic pressure
- there is a net inward force due to water potential
- water is drawn back into the capillaries by osmosis; other substances (such as carbon dioxide) diffuse into the blood down concentration gradients

Plants

Transpiration

The movement of water through a plant is called **transpiration**, although this term is sometimes used to describe just the loss of water from the leaves.

Water moves through a plant in the following ways:
- It moves from one living cell to another (across the roots and leaves) down a water potential gradient, by **osmosis.**
- It moves through the xylem from root to leaf because of a combination of **physical forces**:
  - **root pressure** — a physical upwards push due to more water entering the xylem vessels

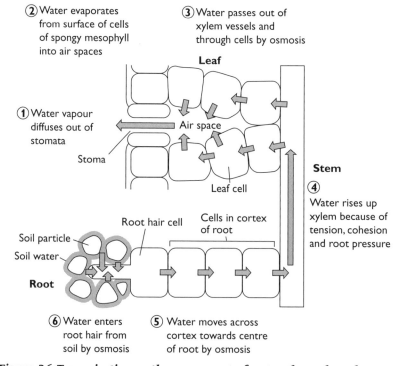

Figure 36 Transpiration — the movement of water through a plant

    – **tension** — a state of negative pressure due to evaporation of water from the leaves (a pull)

    – **cohesion** — an attractive force between water molecules due to hydrogen bonding

- It **evaporates** from the surfaces of cells in the spongy mesophyll into the air spaces.
- It **diffuses** down a water potential gradient from the air spaces of the spongy mesophyll of the leaf, through open stomata and into the atmosphere.

How does water enter and move across the root?

Water enters the root epidermal cells, particularly the root hair cells (which increase the surface area available for absorption), by osmosis down a water potential gradient. A water potential gradient also exists across the root; the epidermal cells have a higher (less negative) water potential than cells in the centre of the root. Therefore, water moves, by osmosis, through the cortex towards the centre of the root where the xylem is found.

There are two main pathways by which water moves through the root:

- the **symplast** pathway — in this pathway, water moves through the walls, membranes and cytoplasm of the cells
- the **apoplast** pathway — in this pathway, water moves only through the cell walls and intercellular spaces

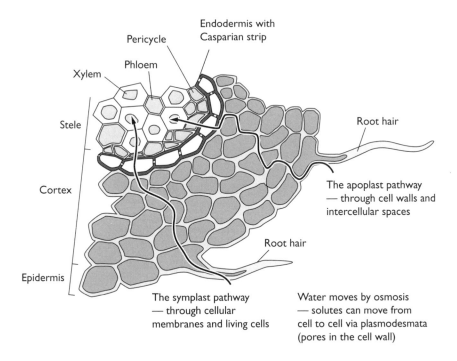

Figure 37 Movement of water across a root

The cells of the endodermis have a layer of suberin (a fatty substance) called the **Casparian strip** in their walls. This acts as an apoplast block, preventing water from moving through the cell walls of the endodermal cells.

Cells surrounding the xylem elements in the root secrete ions into the **xylem**, reducing their water potential. Water then follows by osmosis. As more and more water enters the xylem in the centre of the root, it creates a 'root pressure', which forces the water up the xylem.

Water is lost from the leaves because a water potential gradient exists from the xylem in the leaf ($\Psi \approx -0.5$ MPa) to the leaf cells ($\Psi \approx -1.5$ MPa) to the air spaces ($\Psi \approx -10$ MPa) and finally to the atmosphere ($\Psi \approx -13$ to -120 MPa). When the guard cells open the stomata, water moves down this water potential gradient.

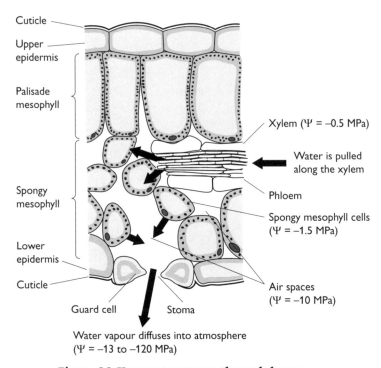

Cuticle

Upper epidermis

Palisade mesophyll

Xylem ($\Psi = -0.5$ MPa)

Water is pulled along the xylem

Spongy mesophyll

Phloem

Spongy mesophyll cells ($\Psi = -1.5$ MPa)

Lower epidermis

Cuticle

Air spaces ($\Psi = -10$ MPa)

Guard cell   Stoma

Water vapour diffuses into atmosphere ($\Psi = -13$ to -120 MPa)

Figure 38 How water moves through leaves

Water moves up the stems in the xylem vessels, which form continuous narrow tubes from roots to leaves, because of:
- the loss of water from the xylem in the leaves, which creates a tension (negative pressure) at the top of the water column in the xylem
- the cohesive force between the water molecules, which is stronger than the force of the tension

The water molecules effectively form a continuous column, so as the 'top end' is pulled upwards, the rest of the column follows. The root pressure, due to more water entering the xylem in the roots, also helps by giving a 'push'. However, most of the force comes from the tension created by the loss of water from the leaves.

> **Tip** Think of sucking water through a straw; your 'suck' creates a negative pressure (tension) and the cohesive forces between the water molecules ensure that a column of water passes up the straw and into your mouth.

Factors affecting the rate of transpiration can be grouped into two categories:
- those that affect the water potential gradient between the air spaces in the spongy mesophyll and the atmosphere
- those that affect the total stomatal aperture (effectively, this represents the surface area available for diffusion)

Factors affecting the water potential gradient include:
- atmospheric humidity. A high concentration of water vapour in the atmosphere will reduce the water potential gradient between air spaces in the leaf and the atmosphere. The rate of transpiration will be reduced.
- atmospheric temperature. When temperature increases, the water vapour molecules have more kinetic energy; they move faster away from the stomata as they escape. The rate of transpiration increases.
- Wind moves water vapour away from the stomata as they escape. This decreases the water potential of the atmosphere and increases the water potential gradient. The rate of transpiration increases.

> **Tip** Everyone knows that clothes on a washing line dry best when it is warm, dry and windy. The same applies to plants.

Factors affecting total stomatal aperture include:
- number of stomata. The more stomata there are per unit area of leaf epidermis, the greater the total aperture and the greater the rate of transpiration.
- light intensity. A rise in light intensity opens stomata, increasing the total aperture and so increasing the rate of transpiration.

Measuring the rate of transpiration
The rate of transpiration can be measured using a **potometer**.

There are two basic types of potometer (Figure 39):
- The bubble potometer measures the rate of water **uptake** by a plant by timing how quickly a bubble in a column of water moves a certain distance along capillary tubing (of known diameter) attached to the plant.
- The mass potometer measures the water loss from a plant by measuring the change in mass over a period of time.

The leafy shoot should be placed in the apparatus under water so that no unwanted air bubbles are introduced.

The first design of bubble potometer is easier to assemble and cheaper, but repeat readings are difficult to obtain as the apparatus must be re-assembled each time. The second apparatus allows repeat readings to be taken easily. After each reading, more

Bubble potometer

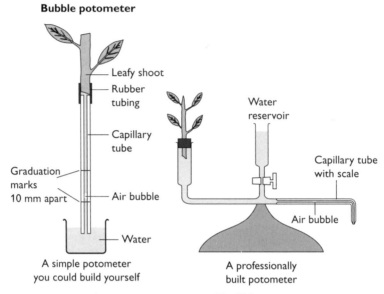

Leafy shoot
Rubber tubing
Capillary tube
Graduation marks
10 mm apart
Air bubble
Water

Water reservoir
Capillary tube with scale
Air bubble

A simple potometer
you could build yourself

A professionally
built potometer

Figure 39 Two types of bubble potometer

water is run into the apparatus from the reservoir, pushing the air bubble back to the end of the capillary tube, ready for another reading to be taken.

Both versions measure water uptake, which is assumed to be directly related to water loss by transpiration.

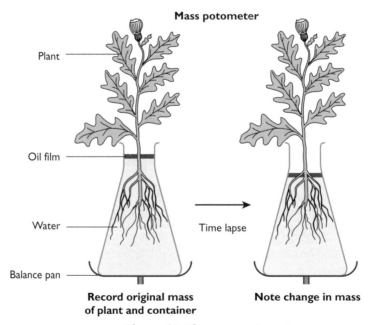

Mass potometer

Plant

Oil film

Water   Time lapse

Balance pan

**Record original mass
of plant and container**

Note change in mass

Figure 40 The mass potometer

The apparatus in Figure 40 does actually measure the amount of water lost, rather than the amount taken up. However, its accuracy is limited by the accuracy of the balance used to measure the mass.

The assumption in this apparatus is that water loss from the plant accounts for the entire loss in mass. Some loss in mass could be due to losses through the oil film.

What the examiners could ask you to do

- Explain any of the key concepts.
- Recall and show understanding of any of the key facts.
- Interpret data on experiments concerning transpiration under different conditions.
- Interpret data on gas exchange in familiar and unfamiliar organisms.
- Interpret data relating body size and shape to gas exchange in terms of surface area-to-volume ratio.

Different cells in different organisms

Key facts you must know and understand

Different types of cells

When compared with eukaryotic cells, prokaryotic cells:

- are usually much smaller
- do not have a true nucleus (the DNA is not contained within a nuclear envelope)
- do not have membrane-bound organelles (lysosomes, mitochondria and chloroplasts)
- have circular DNA (the DNA forms a closed loop rather than a linear molecule)
- have 'naked' DNA (the DNA is not associated with proteins in chromosomes)
- have plasmids (very small circular bits of DNA)
- have cell walls made of peptidoglycan (not cellulose like plant cell walls)
- sometimes have a 'capsule' outside the cell wall

Plant and animal cells are both eukaryotic, but still show some differences, as shown in the following table.

Structure	Structure present or absent in:	
	Plant cell	Animal cell
Cell wall	Present	Absent
Plasma membrane	Present	Present
Nucleus	Present	Present
Chloroplast	Present	Absent
Vacuole	Present	Absent

If we consider a palisade mesophyll cell from a leaf, and an epithelial cell from the small intestine, we can see some of these differences, even through an optical microscope.

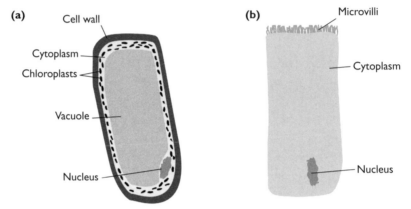

Figure 41 (a) The structure of a palisade mesophyll cell and (b) the structure of an epithelial cell from the small intestine, as seen through an optical microscope

Key structures in plant cells

The cell wall

The cell wall of a plant is a complex structure with several layers. A cell wall always contains:

- a middle lamella — made from pectins
- a primary wall — made from cellulose, hemicelluloses and pectin

It may also contain:

- a secondary wall — this may be made from different substances; in xylem cells it is made from lignin

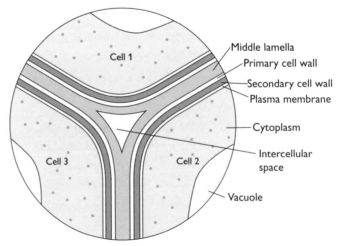

Figure 42 Layers in a cell wall

The cellulose molecules are organised into microfibrils (see page 60), and then into fibres. The fibres in the cell wall run in different directions, conferring greater strength than if they all ran in the same direction, whilst still allowing some elasticity.

Gaps between the cellulose fibres ensure that the cell wall is freely permeable to molecules of all sizes.

The other molecules in the primary wall, pectins and hemi-celluloses, help to hold the cellulose fibres in place.

The lignin in the secondary cell wall of some xylem cells called xylem vessels makes the cell wall much more rigid and harder than the cell walls of other plant cells.

The extra rigidity of xylem vessels (due to the lignin in its secondary cell wall) is important in resisting the inward force of the tension produced by transpiration and is one adaptation to its function of transporting water through a plant. Other adaptations are as follows:

- Xylem vessels are hollow; they 'die' soon after they are formed; all the cytoplasm and organelles are lost.
- The end walls of the cell break down.

These adaptations allow them to form continuous hollow tubes that run throughout the plant, transporting water from root to leaf.

Tip Think how a straw collapses inwards if you suck too hard. Xylem vessels do not do that.

The cell wall of guard cells also adapts them to their function. The wall is thicker in some places than others. When the guard cells take in water by osmosis, they swell. The inner, thicker region of the wall cannot stretch and so the outer region stretches more and the guard cells curve and open the stoma.

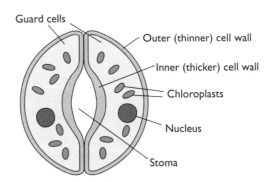

Guard cells
Outer (thinner) cell wall
Inner (thicker) cell wall
Chloroplasts
Nucleus
Stoma

Figure 43 Diagram of guard cells

Chloroplasts
Cells that contain chloroplasts can photosynthesise. The ultrastructure of a chloroplast is linked to harnessing light energy to drive chemical reactions.

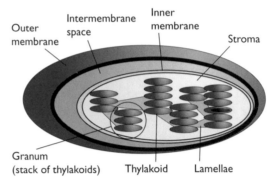

Figure 44 Diagram of a chloroplast

The thylakoid membranes contain chlorophyll and other pigments arranged in such a way that:
- the pigments absorb light energy efficiently
- the energy is used to synthesise ATP and to split water into hydrogen ions, electrons and oxygen
- the hydrogen ions join to an acceptor molecule

The chemical reactions of photosynthesis take place in the liquid stroma; here:
- carbon dioxide enters a complex cycle of reactions that synthesise glucose
- the hydrogen acceptor molecule and ATP 'drive' this cycle of reactions

Different human cells
The many different types of human cells arise from **cellular differentiation**. Following fertilisation, the zygote divides repeatedly by mitosis to form a hollow ball of cells with a group of cells at one end called the inner cell mass. This inner cell mass will eventually give rise to nearly all the different adult cells. It first gives rise to three layers of cells:
- endoderm — the inner layer
- mesoderm — the middle layer
- ectoderm — the outer layer

Through a complex signalling system, the cells in different positions in the embryo develop in different ways into different tissues. Figure 45 shows some of these.

Tissues, organs and organ systems
Tissues
A tissue is a group of similar cells that all perform the same function. Some examples of tissues are described below.

Epithelium is a layer of cells that covers a body part of an animal. Usually it consists of a single layer of cells sitting on a thin, glycoprotein 'basement membrane'. If the epithelium lines an organ, it may be referred to as an **endothelium**. Unlike many other types of cell, most epithelial cells retain the ability to divide. This is important because cells that line or cover structures are continuously worn away and have to be replaced.

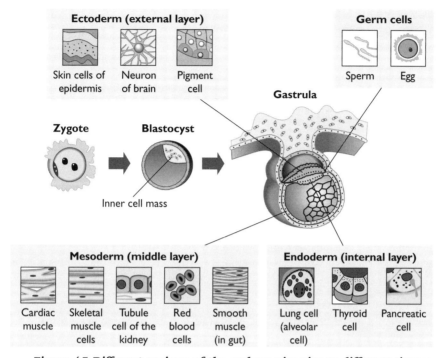

Figure 45 Different regions of the embryo give rise to different tissues

Cells of **squamous epithelium** are extremely thin. They are found:
- in the lungs, where they form the walls of the alveoli and aid gas exchange by contributing to the short diffusion pathway
- lining arteries, where they provide a smooth inner lining to the wall of the artery, reducing resistance to the flow of blood

The **columnar epithelium** cells lining the small intestine have **microvilli** to increase the surface area for uptake of nutrients.

Connective tissue consists of relatively few specialised cells in a non-cellular matrix that contains protein fibres.

Bone and cartilage are typical examples of connective tissue. The non-cellular matrix of bone contains calcium salts that confer hardness. Different types of cartilage contain different proportions of protein fibres. This results in varying degrees of elasticity or rigidity.

Blood can be thought of as a kind of connective tissue in which the plasma is the non-cellular matrix and the blood cells are the specialised cells. Blood has more than one function, so there is more than one type of cell.

Other animal tissues include muscle and nervous tissue.

Plant tissues include spongy mesophyll, palisade mesophyll, epidermis, xylem and phloem.

Organs and organ systems

Organs are structures within an organism that are made of several types of tissue. Each tissue performs its own function and is essential to the overall functioning of the organ.

A muscle (such as the biceps) is an organ. It contains **skeletal muscle tissue**, together with arteries and veins (each made from epithelia, smooth muscle and connective tissue), blood and nervous tissue.

A nerve (such as the vagus nerve) contains mainly **nervous tissue**, but also contains blood vessels, blood and connective tissue.

> **Tip** Be clear in your mind about the difference between a muscle and muscle tissue (also a nerve and nervous tissue). A muscle contains muscle tissue, but other tissues as well and is therefore an organ.

Arteries and veins are also organs because they contain several types of tissue. However, capillaries contain only endothelial tissue and so cannot be classified as organs.

A leaf is a plant organ containing:
- upper and lower **epidermis**, to protect the leaf from damage, infection and dehydration; the lower epidermis also allows gas exchange
- **palisade mesophyll** — the main photosynthetic layer, with columnar cells (allowing tight packing), each containing many chloroplasts to ensure maximum light absorption
- **spongy mesophyll**, to allow diffusion of gases in both directions between the atmosphere (via the stomata) and the palisade layer
- veins containing:
  - **xylem** to transport water to the leaf
  - **phloem** to transport organic substances to and from the leaf

Major body processes are not usually performed by single organs but by groups of organs working together forming an **organ system**.

The circulatory system comprises the heart, arteries, veins and capillaries.

The breathing system comprises the lungs, trachea, larynx and nasal cavity, as well as the diaphragm and intercostal muscles that make breathing movements possible.

What the examiners could ask you to do

- Explain any of the key concepts.
- Recall and show understanding of any of the key facts.
- Interpret information on cellular function to identify adaptations of the cells.
- Identify structures as tissues, organs or organ systems.
- Relate the structure of cell wall and chloroplast to their functions.

Different molecules in different organisms

Differences in DNA between cells of different organisms can lead to different molecules being synthesised, as shown in the diagram below.

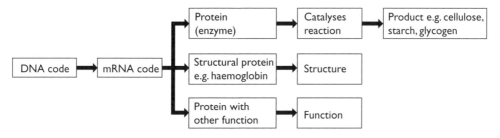

Figure 46 DNA differences can produce different molecules

Key concepts you must understand

Haemoglobin

Haemoglobin is a protein with a quaternary structure; it is composed of four polypeptide chains, linked together to form a single molecule.

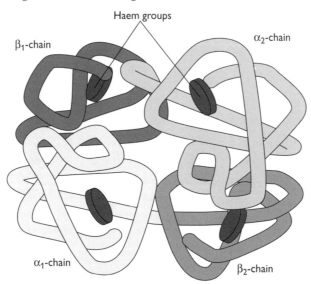

Figure 47 The quaternary structure of haemoglobin

Haemoglobin can bind loosely with oxygen to form **oxyhaemoglobin**; this dissociates easily again to release the oxygen.

The percentage of haemoglobin that has oxygen bound is referred to as the **percentage saturation** of haemoglobin. Figure 48 shows how the percentage satura-tion varies with the partial pressure of oxygen surrounding the red cell containing the haemoglobin, and is referred to as the **dissociation curve of haemoglobin**.

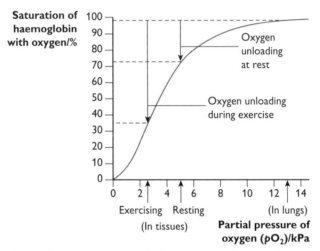

Figure 48 Oxygen dissociation curve of human haemoglobin

The difference in saturation between the lungs (98%) and the tissues varies depending on activity, and is due to oxygen dissociating from the haemoglobin and being released to the tissues.

The precise structure of haemoglobin depends on the DNA that codes for the amino acid sequences. This differs slightly between organisms and so the different haemo-globins have different properties.

Different haemoglobins have different affinities for oxygen because of their structures. The affinity can also be altered by environmental factors, such as pH and the concen-tration of carbon dioxide.

The difference in storage carbohydrates in plants and animals is related to the differ-ence in metabolic rates. Animals have a higher metabolic rate and so must be able to hydrolyse their storage carbohydrate more rapidly than plants.

Key facts you must know and understand

The haemoglobin of animals that live in conditions of low partial pressures of oxygen has a higher affinity for oxygen than normal human haemoglobin, for example:
- on high mountains (the llama)
- in burrows that fill with water (arenicola — a worm that lives in the intertidal zone)
- in the womb (fetal haemoglobin has a much higher affinity for oxygen than adult haemoglobin)

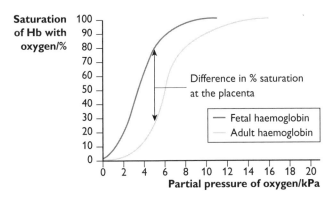

Figure 49 The oxygen dissociation curves of a human fetus and an adult

The dissociation curve of fetal haemoglobin is shifted to the left of the adult haemo-globin curve. This means that it is more highly saturated with oxygen at all partial pressures of oxygen.

At the placenta only 30% of maternal haemoglobin can remain as oxyhaemoglobin. The remaining 70% must release its oxygen. The oxygen diffuses across the placenta and binds with fetal haemoglobin, which can be fully saturated under the same conditions.

When animals are very active, the increased concentration of carbon dioxide in the plasma decreases the pH, which decreases the affinity of haemoglobin for oxygen and more oxygen is released from the oxyhaemoglobin as a result. The dissociation curve is shifted to the right.

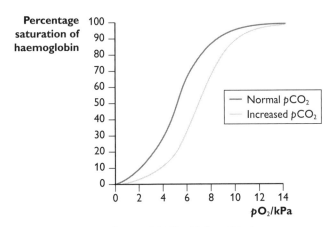

Figure 50 The Bohr effect

This is called the Bohr effect and the result of this is to release more oxygen to tissues than under normal, resting conditions.

Cellulose, starch and glycogen

Cellulose

Cellulose is a structural carbohydrate consisting of many β-glucose molecules joined by condensation reactions to produce an unbranched chain.

Cellulose molecules lying side by side can hydrogen bond themselves into structures called **micelles**. Micelles are grouped into **microfibrils** and these, in turn, are grouped into larger **fibres** of cellulose.

(a) H$_2$COH β-Glucose

(b) β-1,4 linkage

Figure 51 (a) Structure of β-glucose (b) The structure of a cellulose fibre

The fibres of cellulose are used in the synthesis of plant cell walls.

Starch

Starch contains two polymers of α-glucose:

- amylose — an unbranched chain of α-glucose molecules linked by α-1,4 glycosidic bonds
- amylopectin — a branched chain of α-glucose molecules; in the main chains, molecules are linked by α-1,4 glycosidic bonds, as in amylose, but some α-1,6 glycosidic bonds also occur and these form the branch points.

(a)

α-1,4 linkage

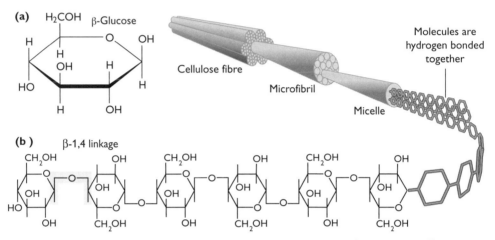

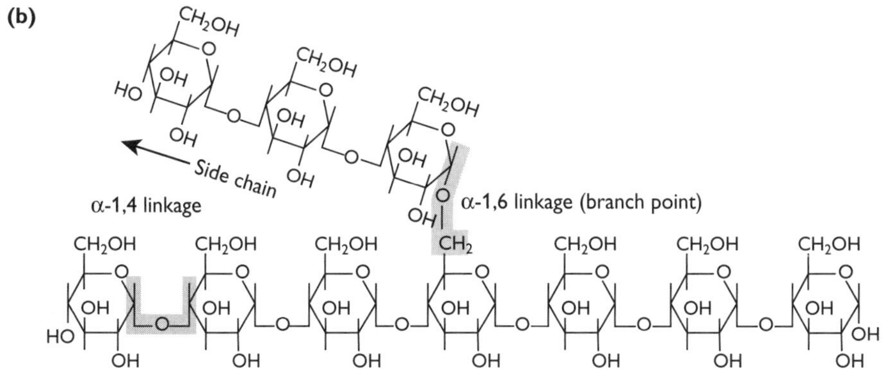

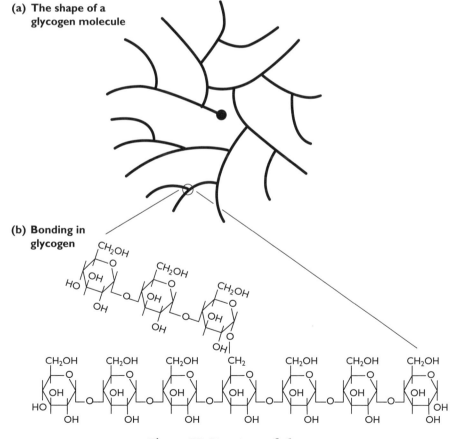

(b)

α-1,4 linkage

Side chain

α-1,6 linkage (branch point)

Figure 52 (a) Structure of amylose (b) Structure of amylopectin

(a) The shape of a glycogen molecule

(b) Bonding in glycogen

Figure 53 Structure of glycogen

Starch is an effective storage carbohydrate because:

- amylose is a compact molecule, so much can be packed into a starch grain in a cell
- amylopectin is rapidly hydrolysed to glucose, because enzymes can begin to operate on all 'ends' of the branches
- both are insoluble, which means that they will have no osmotic effect on surrounding cells

Glycogen
Animals also need to store carbohydrate but, because of their higher metabolic rate, need to be able to 'access' the store quickly. This means that their storage product must be capable of even more rapid hydrolysis. Glycogen is a very highly branched molecule — much more branched than amylopectin (Figure 53 on page 61).

What the examiners could ask you to do

- Explain any of the key concepts.
- Recall and show understanding of any of the key facts.
- Interpret dissociation curves of haemoglobin to deduce the likely conditions producing the curve or the type of haemoglobin present.
- Identify a carbohydrate molecule from drawings provided.

Classifying organisms

Key concepts you must understand

Classification systems
Some classification systems of organisms are **artificial classifications**, others are **natural classifications**. They differ in some important ways.

Artificial systems are built on *conveniently observed features*, and groups are *constructed* using the presence or absence of these features. For example, both tarantula and cobra could be placed in the artificial group of 'poisonous animals'. Owls and eagles are both 'birds of prey', but they belong to different natural groups.

Natural systems seek to *discover* groups that exist *as a result of evolution* by looking at as many features of the organisms as possible, with the aim of establishing true 'kinship' between organisms. For example, the different groups of vertebrate animals seem to be natural groups that are the product of evolution.

Placing organisms in groups based on their evolutionary history is called **phylogeny**. **Phylogenetic trees** show how different organisms have evolved at different times from a common ancestor. Figure 54 shows a phylogenetic tree for some of the main groups of organisms. To compare how closely related groups are, the common branching point must be found. The further back this is, the less closely related the groups are.

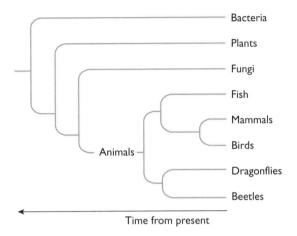

Figure 54 A phylogenetic tree

The different groups in a classification system are called **taxons** and the study of classification is called **taxonomy**. Modern classification systems are hierarchical, with several related smaller taxa being included in a larger taxon.

> **Tip** Think of Russian dolls with each Russian doll containing one smaller doll; however, a classification group probably contains several groups of the 'next size down'.

Key facts you must know and understand

The hierarchy of taxa in one current classification system is:
- **Kingdom**
- **Phylum**
- **Class**
- **Order**
- **Family**
- **Genus**
- **Species**

All organisms have a double-barrelled scientific name. It is called a **binomial**. All cats have the same 'first name' or **generic** name (*Felis*) — this is the genus to which they belong. The last name (**specific** name) is different for each species. *Felis catus* is the domestic cat, *Felis sylvestris*, the European wild cat and *Felis lynx*, the lynx. Modern humans are *Homo sapiens*.

Besides the cats mentioned above, there are other 'cat-like' mammals such as lions, tigers, cheetahs and leopards. The scientific name of the lion is *Panthera leo*. It is in the genus *Panthera* (the panthers). The cheetah, *Acinonyx jubatus*, is from a different genus. However, because these big cats and the smaller cats are really quite similar, they are all placed into one larger group, the **family** of cats — the Felidae.

Cats are clearly different from dogs, yet there *are* similarities. They are both carnivorous mammals and so are grouped into the order Carnivora within the class Mammalia. Mammals belong to the phylum Chordata, which includes all the vertebrates. Finally, chordates belong to the kingdom Animalia.

There are five kingdoms in this classification system:

Kingdom	Organisms included	Main features of organisms
Animalia	All animals	Multicellular, develop from a blastocyst, have eukaryotic cells, usually motile, usually ingest food into a digestive system
Plantae	All plants	Multicellular, eukaryotic cells with cellulose cell walls, photosynthetic
Fungi	All fungi	Eukaryotic cells, some unicells but most multicellular, non-photosynthetic, cell walls made of chitin, secrete enzymes to digest food
Prokaryotae	Bacteria and blue-green bacteria	Prokaryotic cells with no true nuclei, no membrane-bound organelles, circular DNA, peptidoglycan cell walls
Protoctista	Everything else	Eukaryotic cells, may be motile with no cell walls; may be photosynthetic with non-cellulose cell walls

Key concepts you must understand

The species concept

The smallest taxon is the species. Several related species are grouped into the next taxon, the genus, and so on. A species is often defined as: 'An interbreeding group of organisms that produces viable and fertile offspring which share a common ancestry and are similar in anatomy and biochemistry'.

However, this definition has limitations:

- What about species that reproduce asexually? Interbreeding to form viable and fertile offspring cannot occur.
- Some organisms, apparently within one 'species', may be very similar to others, but have different reproductive patterns and so, again, cannot produce viable and fertile offspring.
- Different populations within a species may show some anatomical and physiological differences and may inhabit different geographical or ecological areas. For example, there are two distinct 'sub-species' of the African cheetah.
- The concept cannot easily be applied to fossils.

Some biologists suggest including other criteria in the species concept. These include:

- a common mate recognition system (courtship ritual). This would exclude from a species individuals that appear similar to other individuals, but are **reproductively isolated** from them.
- exploiting the same ecological niche. This is based on the idea that the demands of one particular niche would select out just one type to be successful.

Key concepts you must understand

New techniques used to classify organisms

DNA hybridisation

This technique measures the extent of similarity between two DNA samples. DNA samples that are very similar share many genes and, therefore, many features. They are likely to come from closely related organisms.

The technique measures the extent to which strands of the DNA molecules from the two samples can bind with each other (hybridise).

Protein analysis

Proteins are coded for by DNA. Therefore, similar proteins in two species imply similar DNA. Genetic similarity suggests a close relationship between groups.

Protein analysis aims to compare amino acid sequences of the same protein in different organisms. The more differences, the less closely related the species are presumed to be. However, although data exist for comparison of haemoglobin sequences from many species, the technique is very time-consuming and another technique based on immune responses has been developed.

If a protein from one organism enters another, antibodies specific to that protein will be produced against it. A protein from a third organism, exposed to the antibodies, will only be fully agglutinated or precipitated by the antibodies if the two proteins are very similar. If the two proteins are dissimilar, the extent of the agglutination will be very different also.

Key facts you must know and understand

DNA hybridisation

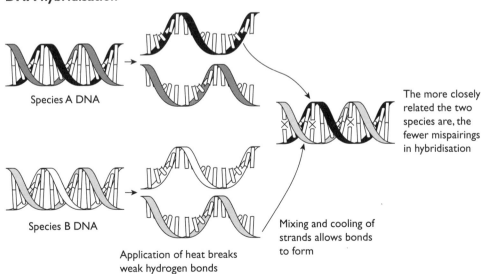

Species A DNA

The more closely related the two species are, the fewer mispairings in hybridisation

Species B DNA

Mixing and cooling of strands allows bonds to form

Application of heat breaks weak hydrogen bonds

Figure 55 Technique of DNA hybridisation

This technique is carried out as follows (see Figure 55 on page 65):
- DNA samples from two different species are heated separately to nearly boiling in order to separate the strands.
- The samples are mixed and allowed to cool.
- Separate strands from the two samples begin to hybridise (re-bind).

Strands from the same species will show 100% hybridisation as they will be completely complementary. Samples from closely related species will show high-percentage hybridisation, whereas it will be lower for more distantly related species.

Using DNA hybridisation techniques, the phylogenetic tree of humans and the great apes appears as in Figure 56.

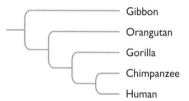

Gibbon

Orangutan

Gorilla

Chimpanzee

Human

Figure 56 The phylogenetic tree of humans and the great apes, based on DNA hybridisation data

Protein analysis

The immune response comparison technique is carried out as follows:
- A protein from species A is injected into an experimental animal. The animal makes antibodies against it.
- Shortly afterwards, the same protein from species B is exposed to the antibodies and the strength of the new agglutination reaction is estimated.
- if the proteins are very similar, the second agglutination reaction will be stronger than if they are only slightly similar.

Using this immunological technique, the phylogenetic tree of humans and the great apes appears slightly different from that obtained with the DNA hybridisation technique.

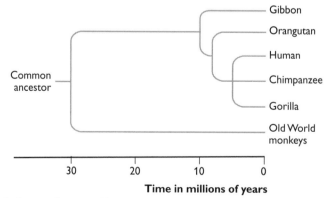

Figure 57 Phylogenetic tree of humans and great apes based on immunological data

What the examiners could ask you to do

- Explain any of the key concepts.
- Recall and show understanding of any of the key facts.
- Complete classifications of organisms, given appropriate data.
- Interpret data from DNA hybridisation or protein analysis and construct phylogenetic trees.
- Interpret phylogenetic trees.

Biodiversity

Key concepts you must understand

Measures of biodiversity

The most usual way to think of biodiversity is in terms of **species richness**. This is quite simply the number of different species that are present in an **ecosystem**.

However, if only one or two individuals of a particular species are present in an ecosystem, they won't be contributing a great deal to the biodiversity of the system. A more useful concept is **species diversity**. This takes into account not just how many different species are present, but also the success of each species in the ecosystem.

An **index of diversity** can be calculated and this can be used to give a picture of the ecosystem as a whole.

The examples below relate to three areas containing the same six species (they have the same species richness) and the same total number of organisms — yet the areas are clearly very different.

Species	Number of organisms of each species		
	Area 1	Area 2	Area 3
A	86	16	23
B	5	17	25
C	2	16	27
D	3	17	5
E	1	17	12
F	3	17	8

The species diversity of the three areas should reflect the difference in abundance of the six species within each area. **Simpson's index of diversity** is calculated from the formula:

$$d = \frac{N(N-1)}{\Sigma n(n-1)}$$

In this formula, d is the index of diversity, N is the total number of organisms in the area and n is the total number of organisms of each species.

For area 1,

$$d = \frac{100 \times 99}{(86 \times 85) + (5 \times 4) + (2 \times 1) + (3 \times 2) + (1 \times 0) + (3 \times 2)} = 1.348$$

For area 2,

$$d = \frac{100 \times 99}{(16 \times 15) + (17 \times 16) + (16 \times 15) + (17 \times 16) + (17 \times 16) + (17 \times 16)} = 6.314$$

For area 3,

$$d = \frac{100 \times 99}{(23 \times 22) + (25 \times 24) + (27 \times 26) + (5 \times 4) + (12 \times 11) + (8 \times 7)} = 4.911$$

A low value for the index of diversity suggests:
- only a few successful species, perhaps only one
- the environment is quite hostile with relatively few ecological niches and only a few organisms are really well adapted to that environment
- food webs that are relatively simple
- change in the environment would probably have quite serious effects

A higher diversity index suggests:
- a number of successful species and a more stable ecosystem
- more ecological niches are available and the environment is likely to be less hostile
- complex food webs
- environmental change is likely to be less damaging to the ecosystem as a whole; tropical rainforests provide an example of a stable ecosystem with high species diversity.

Biodiversity operates on other levels also. Besides species diversity, we should consider:
- genetic diversity — the size of the gene pool of a species (the variety of genes and alleles of a species). If local populations are lost, the genetic diversity will be reduced, even though the overall species diversity remains unaltered.
- ecosystem diversity — an organism may exist in a number of different ecosystems. If one of these is lost, then although that species is not lost (although its gene pool will be reduced), others may be. Certainly, the community of organisms in that ecosystem will be lost. More different ecosystems mean more different habitats and this gives more chance for one species to evolve different varieties.

The impact of human activity on biodiversity
A report by the World Conservation Union concluded that: 'The world's biological diversity is more threatened now than at any time since the extinction of the dinosaurs 65 million years ago'.

Key facts you must know and understand

Deforestation
Deforestation is usually carried out for two main reasons:
- to clear land for human activity, such as mining, agriculture or house building
- to obtain timber to make paper, charcoal, furniture, or as a building material

Tropical rainforest is one of the most complex and species-rich ecosystems in the world. There are several 'layers' to tropical rainforest, as shown in Figure 58.

Figure 58 Structure of a tropical rain forest

Rainforest covers about 7% of the earth's surface and contains 25% of the known species, most of which are found in the canopy and emergents.

Felling tropical rainforest has far-reaching effects:
- There is a serious reduction in species diversity. Many ecological niches are destroyed when trees are felled and the species that fill these niches are lost.
- There is a reduction in the rate at which carbon dioxide is removed from the atmosphere. In addition, if the trees are burned, then carbon dioxide is added to the atmosphere.
- There is a reduction in the amount of nitrogen returned to the soil as much of the timber is taken from the area or burned. Any tree trunks not removed from the area are slow to decay and the soil is depleted in nitrate for many years.
- If the felled area is allowed to regenerate, shrubs are often the first plants to grow and these out-compete the slower-growing trees for mineral ions and light. The area may not return to a rainforest ecosystem, but a much less complex one.

The felling of trees need not be totally destructive and the practice need not be halted. However, the rainforests must be conserved, and felling and re-planting in a planned cycle over a number of years can do this. This could give a sustainable yield of timber, without endangering the species diversity of the rainforests.

Agricultural practices

Large areas of land given over to the production of just one crop plant (such as maize or another cereal) inevitably bring a reduction in biodiversity for several reasons, including:
- the area is dominated by just one species, drastically reducing the number of niches for other organisms to fill

- organisms that might live there are regarded as pests as they reduce the crop yield and are controlled by pesticides
- hedgerows are removed to create bigger, more productive fields; this reduces still further the number of habitats and niches, and therefore the biodiversity of the area
- wetlands are drained to create land for the same reason

Other agricultural practices reducing biodiversity include:
- the widespread use of fertilisers to maintain soil fertility; these can run off into nearby waterways causing eutrophication, a process that leads to the water becoming anoxic (lacking oxygen)
- some species are culled or hunted because of their impact on livestock (e.g. badgers and foxes)
- growing more than one crop per year in the same field means that the field almost never has 'stubble' growing, which can be a valuable habitat
- crop rotation is no longer practised.

Traditionally, crops were rotated so that in a particular field a cereal would be grown one year, then perhaps a root crop such as carrots, then a legume such as beans and then perhaps one year 'fallow' (just grass, no crop). The rotation would be carried out with different timings in different fields, so that all crops were always available. This meant that different animals could find different habitats.

Field A	Field B			
Field C	Field D			

Field	Crop			
	Year 1	Year 2	Year 3	Year 4
A	Root	Legume	Fallow	Cereal
B	Cereal	Root	Legume	Fallow
C	Fallow	Cereal	Root	Legume
D	Legume	Fallow	Cereal	Root

Figure 59 Crop rotation

What the examiners could ask you to do

- Explain any of the key concepts.
- Recall and show understanding of any of the key facts.
- Calculate an index of diversity from data supplied.
- Interpret data concerning the effects of deforestation or agricultural practices.
- Discuss the ways in which information concerning loss in biodiversity could be interpreted by different interested parties.

Questions
&
Answers

This section contains questions similar in style to those you can expect to see in your Unit 2 examination. The limited number of questions in this guide means that it is impossible to cover all the topics and all the question styles, but they should give you a flavour of what to expect. The responses that are shown are real students' answers to the questions.

There are several ways of using this section. You could:

- 'hide' the answers to each question and try the question yourself. It needn't be a memory test — use your notes to see if you can actually make all the points you ought to make
- check your answers against the candidates' responses and make an estimate of the likely standard of your response to each question
- check your answers against the examiner's comments to see where you might have lost marks
- check your answers against the terms used in the question — for example, did you *explain* when you were asked to, or did you merely *describe*?

Examiner's comments

All candidate responses are followed by examiner's comments. These are preceded by the icon *e* and indicate where credit is due. In the weaker answers, they also point out areas for improvement, specific problems, and common errors such as lack of clarity, weak or non-existent development, irrelevance, misinterpretation of the question and mistaken meanings of terms.

The structure and function of DNA

(a) Figure 1 represents the structure of the DNA molecule.

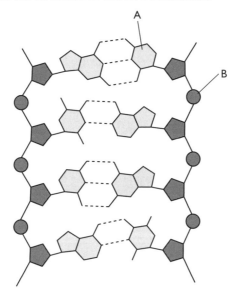

Figure 1

  (i) Name the structures labelled **A** and **B**.   (2 marks)

 (ii) Use the diagram to explain why the **DNA** molecule is sometimes described as consisting of two polynucleotide strands.   (1 mark)

(b) 15% of the bases in a sample of **DNA** are adenine. What percentage will be guanine? Explain your answer.   (2 marks)

Total: 5 marks

■ ■ ■

Candidates' answers to Question 1

Candidate A
(a) (i) A — nucleotide; B — phosphorus

Candidate B
(a) (i) A is a nitrogenous base (adenine, thymine, cytosine or guanine);
B is a phosphate group which links adjacent nucleotides.

   ✍ Candidate A is clearly confused between nucleotide and nitrogenous base — make sure you aren't, it's not a difficult question. Phosphorus is a chemical element and so is not an acceptable answer as B is a phosphate group. Candidate A scores no marks. Candidate B is clearly familiar with the components of a DNA molecule and is awarded both marks.

Candidate A
(a) (ii) There are two strands with lots of nucleotides joined.

Candidate B
(a) (ii) Each strand consists of many nucleotides linked by the phosphate groups. 'Poly-' means many, like in a polygon.

 Both candidates clearly understand the idea, for 1 mark.

Candidate A
(b) 15%. They are complementary bases.

Candidate B
(b) 15% adenine is complementary to thymine, so there will be 15% thymine also. This adds up to 30%. So 70% will be cytosine and guanine together. They are complementary bases, so there will be equal amounts of each. 70/2 = 35.

 Candidate A understands the basis of the question, but has mistakenly associated adenine with guanine and so loses both marks. Candidate B has the correct answer, which is explained clearly and scores both marks.

 This is a straightforward question, testing basic understanding of the structure of DNA. Despite this, Candidate A scores only 1 of the 5 marks, whereas Candidate B scores all 5. Examiners would expect most candidates to score highly on this question.

Question 2

Biodiversity

In an investigation into two areas, the numbers of several types of plant were recorded. The results are shown in the table below.

Plant species	Number of plants (n) in area A	Number of plants (n) in area B
Woodrush	4	2
Holly	8	3
Bramble	3	3
Yorkshire fog	6	12
Sedge	7	4
Buttercup	7	4
Total (N)	35	28

(a) Use the formula

$$d = \frac{N(N-1)}{\Sigma n(n-1)}$$

to calculate the diversity index for each area. (3 marks)

(b) Give three deductions that might be made about an area with a low diversity index. (3 marks)

(c) Explain *two* ways in which agricultural practices can reduce biodiversity. (4 marks)

Total: 10 marks

■ ■ ■

Candidates' answers to Question 2

Candidate A

(a) For area A,

$$d = \frac{N(N-1)}{\Sigma n(n-1)} = \frac{35 \times 34}{(4 \times 3) + (8 \times 7) + (3 \times 2) + (6 \times 5) + (7 \times 6) + (7 \times 6)} = 6.33$$

Area B

$$= \frac{28 \times 27}{(2 \times 1) + (3 \times 2) + (3 \times 2) + (12 \times 11) + (4 \times 4) + (4 \times 4)} = 4.25$$

Candidate B

(a) The index of diversity for Area A is 6.33. The index for Area B is 4.45.

✍ There is 1 mark here for each correct answer and 1 mark for evidence of a correct method. Candidate B has both answers correct and so must have used a correct method. All 3 marks are awarded. Candidate A clearly understands how to carry out the procedure, but in the second calculation has made a slip. The last two items of the divisor should be (4 x 3) and not (4 x 4) as written. This gives a wrong answer and that mark is obviously lost. However, by showing the correct method, Candidate A is credited with the 'working mark' and scores 2 of the 3. Had Candidate B made the same slip, he/she would probably only have scored 1 mark, as no working is shown.

Candidate A

(b) A low index of diversity means that the area does not have many species present. Therefore it will only have simple food chains and if something alters the environment, the whole ecosystem might collapse.

Candidate B

(b) A low index of diversity indicates an area dominated by just a few species. The area could be quite hostile and the ecosystem unstable.

Both candidates seem to have an understanding of the problem, however Candidate A's first statement is debatable. There could be a good number of species present. It is the idea of the area being dominated by only a few that is not made clear. Candidate A scores 2 marks and Candidate B all 3 marks.

Candidate A

(c) Creating large fields growing just one crop reduces biodiversity because there are fewer habitats and crop rotation does also.

Candidate B

(c) Removing hedgerows reduces the number of habitats. Also, clearing wetlands reduces biodiversity

Candidate A scores 2 marks. The explanation of why monoculture reduces habitats is clear, but crop rotation does not reduce biodiversity. Stopping crop rotation reduces biodiversity. Perhaps this is what the candidate meant, but an examiner can only mark what is written. Candidate B scores 3 marks for correctly identifying two ways in which agricultural practice reduces biodiversity, but the second way is not explained.

Candidate A scores 6 marks overall, but with a little more care and attention to detail could probably have scored more. The slip in the calculation in (a) and careless wording in (c) cost at least 2 marks. Candidate B scores 9 of the 10 marks, and should have scored all ten.

uestion

Mitosis and meiosis

Figure 1 shows a cell in a stage of mitosis. The cell contains just two pairs of homologous chromosomes.

Figure 1

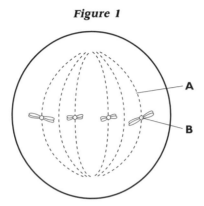

(a) (i)   What are *homologous chromosomes*?   (1 mark)
    (ii) Identify the structures labelled A and B on Figure 1.   (2 marks)
    (iii) Name the stage of mitosis represented in this diagram. Give a
          reason for your answer.   (1 mark)

Figure 2 shows the life cycle of a mammal.

Figure 2

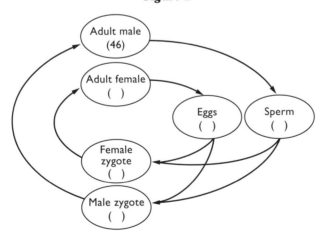

(b) (i) Mark on the diagram one stage where meiosis takes place and one
         place where mitosis takes place.   (2 marks)
    (ii) Complete the empty boxes to show the number of chromosomes
         per cell.   (1 mark)

Total: 7 marks

questions & answers

question

Candidates' answers to Question 3

Candidate A
(a) (i) They have the same genes.

Candidate B
(a) (i) A homologous pair of chromosomes is a pair of chromosomes that have the same genes along their length (although they may not have the same alleles).

> Both candidates score the mark but Candidate B has written much more than is necessary. Just answer the question, without writing part of it out again.

Candidate A
(a) (ii) A is the spindle; B is a chromosome.

Candidate B
(a) (ii) A is the spindle or, more accurately, one of the spindle fibres.
B is the centromere, which holds the chromatids in a chromosome together.

> Candidate A has not looked carefully enough at label **B** which indicates, precisely, the centromere. Candidate A scores 1 mark. Candidate B scores 2 marks.

Candidate A
(a) (iii) Prophase

Candidate B
(a) (iii) Metaphase

> Candidate A has not revised mitosis effectively. This is a straightforward piece of biological knowledge which any candidate who has prepared thoroughly should know. Only Candidate B scores the mark.

Candidate A
(b) (i) and (ii)

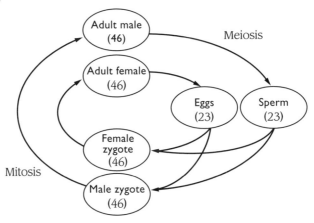

Candidate B

(b) (i) and (ii)

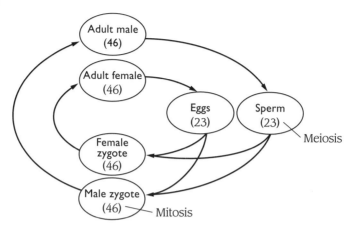

Candidate A is awarded 2 marks for part (b) (i). Candidate B also probably knows exactly where and when the two processes occur, but the labelling is unfortunate. Meiosis does not occur actually in the sperm, so this mark is not awarded. However, the zygote does divide by mitosis and so this mark can be awarded. You will be expected to know that meiosis occurs only in the formation of gametes and that all other cell divisions are by mitosis. You should be able to relate this to a life cycle that you have not studied before. Both candidates understand the halving of chromosomes in the gametes and restoration of the normal (diploid) number in the zygote. Each is awarded the mark for part (b) (ii).

Candidate A scores 5 marks overall, and Candidate B scores 6. It is a fairly straightforward question, demanding recall of some basic knowledge of mitosis and a fairly simple application of the knowledge of mitosis and meiosis to life cycles.

Question 4

Haemoglobin

Oxygen is transported in mammalian blood by the protein haemoglobin in red blood cells. Figure 1 shows the dissociation curve for human haemoglobin at two different pHs.

Figure 1

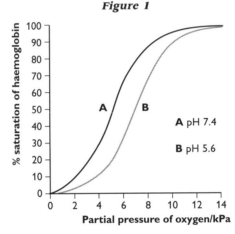

(a) Explain what is meant by 'the percentage saturation of haemoglobin'. (1 mark)

(b) Explain how vigorous exercise could produce a dissociation curve similar to that shown by line B. (2 marks)

(c) Copy the graph and add the dissociation curve you would expect for an animal that lived in an area where the partial pressure of oxygen was low. Explain the curve you have drawn. (3 marks)

Total: 6 marks

■ ■ ■

Candidates' answers to Question 4

Candidate A
(a) The amount of haemoglobin carrying oxygen.

Candidate B
(a) The percentage saturation of haemoglobin is the proportion of haemoglobin in a certain volume of blood that is actually carrying oxygen, that is, oxyhaemoglobin.

> ✏ Both candidates clearly understand the idea of saturation of haemoglobin, but in contrast to Candidate B, Candidate A has not answered precisely enough to score the mark. 'The amount of haemoglobin carrying oxygen' does not convey the idea of proportion. It could mean 10 g or 78 moles or any other amount. Percentage saturation must convey the idea of proportion; 'the amount of haemoglobin bound to oxygen in 100 cm³ of blood' would be acceptable. Read the question carefully.

Candidate A

(b) Vigorous exercise would make the haemoglobin more acidic and so it would not carry oxygen as well. Curve B is lower than curve A.

Candidate B

(b) In vigorous exercise, a lot more carbon dioxide is released from the extra respiration. Carbon dioxide results in carbonic acid forming in the plasma, which will lower the pH of the plasma. Also, lactate (lactic acid) may be produced which would also lower the pH of the plasma. This change in the curve is called the Bohr effect or the Bohr shift.

> 🖉 Candidate A does not really understand that the pHs referred to in the question are plasma pHs and cannot explain how vigorous exercise could change the pH. No marks are awarded. Candidate B gives a very full and clear explanation and is awarded both marks.

Candidate A

(c)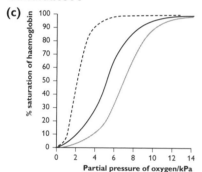

Candidate B

(c)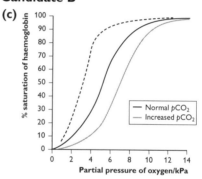

The haemoglobin of animals like the llama has a lower affinity for oxygen than human haemoglobin, so the curve is shifted to the left.

Animals like the llama live on mountains where there is less oxygen. Their haemoglobin has a higher affinity for oxygen than human haemoglobin and so is able to load oxygen even when there is not much around.

> 🖉 Both candidates score 1 mark for the graph. However, Candidate A is clearly confused about high and low affinity haemoglobins and loses that mark. The comment about shifting the curve to the left doesn't add anything new to the graph he/she has drawn. Candidate B explains the situation clearly and scores all 3 marks.

> 🖉 **Candidate A scores only 1 mark while Candidate B scores all 6 for this question. Candidate A has again lost some marks unnecessarily. Although unclear about the concept of 'affinity for oxygen', he/she probably knew that the llama's haemoglobin was adapted to load oxygen under low oxygen tensions and should have said so, rather than just re-stating what had been drawn in the graph. Be careful not to do this.**

Question Q5

Variation

(a) The seeds from several pea plants were collected and weighed. Their masses are shown in the table.

Mass/g	Number of seeds
< 1.0	0
1.1–1.5	1
1.6–2.0	3
2.1–2.5	7
2.6–3.0	11
3.1–3.5	5
3.6–4.0	2
> 4.0	0

(i) Plot a graph of these results.   (3 marks)

(ii) What sort of variation is shown by these data?   (1 mark)

(b) The seeds were germinated in a greenhouse and the heights of the plants at 42 days were measured. The results are shown in the graph.

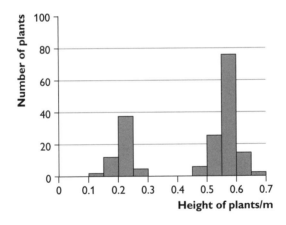

(i) Suggest why the seeds were germinated in a greenhouse rather than in the open.   (2 marks)

(ii) Describe and explain the variation shown between the pea plants.   (4 marks)

Total: 10 marks

Candidates' answers to question 5

Candidate A

(a) (i)

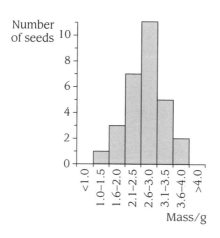

Candidate B

(a) (i)

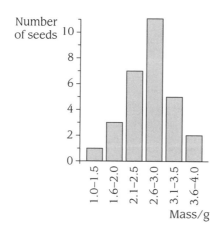

🖉 Both candidates have assigned the *x* and *y* axes correctly, but after that, Candidate B has made several errors and only scores 1 mark. He/she has drawn a bar chart, when a histogram should have been plotted (bars touching, as in Candidate A's graph). Also, Candidate B's graph is incomplete as no values are plotted for <1.0 and >4.0. Both these values are 0, but they should have been plotted. Candidate A draws a histogram with all values plotted correctly and scores 3 marks

Candidate A

(a) (ii) Categoric variation

Candidate B

(a) (ii) Continuous variation

🖉 Candidate B scores 1 mark. Candidate A scores no marks.

question

Candidate A

(b) (i) If you sow the seeds in the open, you don't know what will happen, but in the greenhouse, you can keep it the same temperature all the time.

Candidate B

(b) (i) In a greenhouse, you can control the conditions and so you know that any differences are due to differences in the seeds themselves.

Both candidates have the right idea, but Candidate A expresses this in a very loose way and doesn't explain the consequence of controlling environmental factors, whereas Candidate B makes this clear. Candidate A scores 1 mark (just) whilst Candidate B scores both marks.

Candidate A

(b) (ii) There are two definite groups of seeds, so these probably have different genes. But all the seeds in each group aren't the same. Some could be getting more sunlight than others which would make them photosynthesise better and this would lead to better growth

Candidate B

(b) (ii) There are genetic differences, as there are two distinct groups. But the variation within a group is due to the environment.

Both candidates score all 4 marks for describing the types of variation that exist and explaining how they arrived at their answers. Candidate A was rather 'wordy' in his/her explanation, but it was entirely correct. If you can be concise in your answers, do so — it saves you valuable time in an examination.

Both candidates score 8 marks for this question and both should probably have scored more. Candidate B made silly mistakes in plotting the graph and Candidate A should really have known, after correctly plotting a histogram, that the variation shown was continuous.

Classification

Amoeba proteus and *Paramecium caudatum* are both unicells. They both have eukaryotic cells and are motile.

(a) (i) Copy and complete the table showing the classification of *Amoeba*.

Taxon	Taxonomic group
Kingdom	
	Plasmodroma
	Rhizopoda
	Amoebida
	Amoebidae
Genus	
Species	

(2 marks)

(ii) Name *three* taxa that the two organisms could share.   (1 mark)

(iii) Name *one* taxon that the two organisms do not share.   (1 mark)

(b) Give *two* differences between these cells and bacterial cells.   (2 marks)

Total: 6 marks

■ ■ ■

Candidates' answers to question 6

Candidate A

(a) (i)

Taxon	Taxonomic group
Kingdom	*Animalia*
Phylum	Plasmodroma
Class	Rhizopoda
Order	Amoebida
Family	Amoebidae
Genus	*Amoeba*
Species	*proteus*

question

Candidate B

(a) (i)

Taxon	Taxonomic group
Kingdom	*Protoctista*
Phylum	Plasmodroma
Class	Rhizopoda
Order	Amoebida
Family	Amoebidae
Genus	*Amoeba*
Species	*proteus*

 Candidate A scores 1 mark as the first column in the table is completely correct. However he/she has placed Amoeba in the kingdom Animalia, presumably on the basis that they are motile. Candidate B scores both marks.

Candidate A

(a) (ii) They are both in the Animalia, Plasmodroma and Rhizopoda.

Candidate B

(a) (ii) Kingdom, phylum and order

 Candidate A scores the mark but Candidate B does not — he/she has wrongly suggested order (Amoebida) instead of class (Rhizopoda). Candidate A again suggests Animalia (which is wrong), as well as Plasmodroma and Rhizopoda (which are correct). However, Candidate A was penalised in (a) (i) for Animalia and so is not penalised again here. Candidate A has, effectively, suggested Kingdom, Phylum and Class.

Candidate A

(a) (iii) They are in a different species.

Candidate B

(a) (iii) Species

 Both candidates score the mark.

Candidate A

(b) They have a nucleus and can move.

Candidate B

(b) Eukaryotic cells have true nuclei and membrane-bound organelles, whereas prokaryotic cells don't.

 Candidate A scores only 1 mark, whereas Candidate B scores 2.

 This is a straightforward question on classification and candidates should score well. Candidate A scores 4 marks, Candidate B scores 5.

Genetic bottlenecks

The graph below shows the effect of a genetic bottleneck on the numbers and genetic variability of a population.

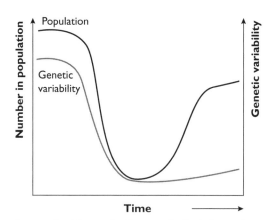

(a) Describe *two* pieces of evidence in the graph that show that a genetic bottleneck took place. (2 marks)

(b) Explain *two* possible reasons for the slight increase in genetic variability after the genetic bottleneck. (4 marks)

(c) Explain why the population after the genetic bottleneck is more vulnerable to environmental change than the population before the bottleneck. (4 marks)

Total: 10 marks

■ ■ ■

Candidates' answers to question 7

Candidate A

(a) The population fell and the genetic variability fell as well.

Candidate B

(a) There was a population crash, but the numbers recovered, whereas the genetic variability fell and stayed low.

> ✓ Candidate B gives a more complete answer than Candidate A, but Candidate A has probably just done enough to score both marks as well.

Candidate A

(b) Mutations would introduce some genetic variability and new combinations of the genes already there would as well.

question

Candidate B

(b) Mutations will actually produce new genes, so increasing the genetic variability. The other way is by random mating and random fertilisation, which will produce new combinations of genes that already exist.

> Both candidates realise the importance of mutations, but only Candidate B explains *how* mutations increase the genetic variability. Candidate A just re-iterates the phrase used in the question. However, in part (b) both candidates make the same mistake of talking about new combinations of genes. All members of the same species will have the same *genes* on the same chromosome; but they may have different *alleles*. The answer should focus on different combinations of *alleles*. Only Candidate B explains how new combinations (of alleles) could happen. Candidate A scores just 1 mark; Candidate B scores 3.

Candidate A

(c) Because there is less variation, if the environment changes, they will either all be suited to the new environment or they all won't.

Candidate B

(c) The lack of genetic variation means that if the environment changes, few if any will be adapted to the new condition and most won't survive.

> Both candidates have grasped the importance of low genetic variability and the consequences of this in terms of adaptation to a new environment. Candidate B goes on to suggest the implications for survival. Candidate A scores 2 marks, Candidate B scores 3.

> **Candidate A scores 5 marks, Candidate B scores 8. This is a question where understanding of concepts is important, but the detail must also be supplied.**

Passing on the genetic material

The graph shows the changes in the amount of DNA in a cell during different stages of the cell cycle.

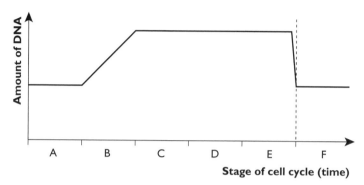

Explain the change in the amount of DNA during:

(a) (i) stage **B** (2 marks)

    (ii) stage **E** (2 marks)

(b) (i) Name the stage of the cell cycle labelled **C**. (1 mark)

    (ii) Describe the events that take place in the stage labelled **A**. (2 marks)

Total: 7 marks

■ ■ ■

Candidates' answers to question 8

Candidate A

(a) (i) The chromosomes had duplicated themselves into chromatids.

Candidate B

(a) (i) This is the S phase of the cell cycle. The DNA undergoes semi-conservative replication.

    ✐ Candidate B scores 2 marks. Candidate A has the right idea — he/she knows that duplication is involved, but doesn't mention DNA at all and scores no marks.

Candidate A

(a) (ii) The cell has divided into two, so some of the DNA ends up in each cell.

Candidate B

(a) (ii) This is cytokinesis and when the cell divides, half the DNA ends up in each cell.

    ✐ Candidate A scores only 1 mark. 'Some' DNA is too vague; it is clear from the data that the amount of DNA is halved. Candidate B describes this accurately and scores both marks.

question

Candidate A

(b) (i) Interphase

Candidate B

(b) (i) G2

> Candidate A's answer is too imprecise — A, B and C collectively form interphase. Candidate B scores 1 mark for a more precise answer.

Candidate A

(b) (ii) In this stage, the cell is getting ready to divide by growing and making more cell structures that can be shared between the cells after cell division.

Candidate B

(b) (ii) In preparation for mitosis, the cell is growing.

> Both candidates have some of the right events, but in the wrong context. The cell grows and synthesises new organelles because these have been reduced by a previous mitotic division. This is the G1 phase of the cycle. Candidate A scores 2 marks for a more complete answer, Candidate B scores just 1.

> **Overall, Candidate A scores 3 marks and Candidate B scores 6 (out of a possible 7 marks). Once again, Candidate A lost marks through a lack of detail and accuracy in the answers.**

Selection in bacteria

The diagram below shows two processes that transfer **DNA** in bacteria.

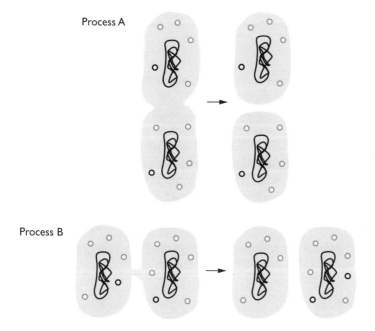

Process A

Process B

(a) (i) Identify each process and state whether it represents
horizontal transmission or vertical transmission. *(4 marks)*
(ii) Describe two ways in which process **A** differs from mitosis. *(2 marks)*

(b) The overuse of antibiotics may be responsible for the increase in the
numbers of bacteria showing resistance to antibiotics. Explain how. *(6 marks)*

(c) Multiple resistance to antibiotics can be acquired by bacteria.
Explain how. *(3 marks)*

Total: 15 marks

■ ■ ■

Candidates' answers to question 9

Candidate A
(a) (i) A is mitosis because one cell just divides into two. B is fertilisation. A is vertical
transmission and B is horizontal transmission.

Candidate B
(a) (i) A — binary fission. This is vertical transmission because it passes from one
generation to the next. B is conjugation, and this is horizontal transmission.

question

📝 Candidate A scores 2 marks for correctly identifying vertical and horizontal transmission, and it rather looks as if these were scored by good luck rather than good management. It is clear from the names given to the processes that this candidate doesn't understand what is happening and has probably guessed the type of transmission. Candidate B clearly understands and scores 4 marks. Mitosis can *never* occur in bacteria, because mitosis is a nuclear division and prokaryotic cells don't have nuclei.

Candidate A
(a) (ii) This process halves the amount of DNA and introduces variation.

Candidate B
(a) (ii) No chromosomes are involved.

📝 When he/she read this question, why did Candidate A not go back to his/her answer to (a) (i) and change it? This question makes clear that process A *can't* be mitosis. This can happen in an examination; one question throws light on the answer to another question, so be on the lookout for it. But, Candidate A is clearly fixed on nuclear divisions and bases his/her answer on differences between mitosis and meiosis, and so scores no marks. Candidate B recognises one essential difference and scores 1 mark, but surprisingly, having got this point, doesn't mention that no nucleus is involved and no spindle is involved.

Candidate A
(b) The bacteria adapt to the use of antibiotics by changing to be resistant to them. This makes them survive better so that more of them are resistant.

Candidate B
(b) Mutations make some of the bacteria resistant to the antibiotic anyway. When the antibiotic is used a lot, these bacteria have an advantage because they won't be killed, so they survive and reproduce.

📝 Both candidates start their answer along the right lines, although Candidate A's answer almost reads as though the bacteria are 'choosing' to adapt. If this is what the examiner believes you are saying, you will lose marks as it is the result of chance mutations — as Candidate B makes clear. Candidate A just about scores 2 marks, whilst Candidate B scores 3. Neither candidate completes the story, however. In answers to questions like this, to score full marks you should address the following:
- the source of the selection pressure (overuse of antibiotics in this case)
- the types that have the advantage (resistant types)
- they will survive and reproduce in greater numbers
- the other forms will survive and reproduce in smaller numbers
- this will repeat over many generations
- the proportion of those with the advantage in the population will increase

Candidate A

(c) Bacteria can swap DNA. So one bacterium can give a resistance gene to another bacterium. If it already had resistance to one antibiotic, it is now resistant to two.

Candidate B

(c) Antibiotic resistance is usually found in genes in plasmids. Bacteria can swap plasmids and transfer resistance to another bacterium.

> Neither candidate mentions conjugation as the process transferring the DNA. The name 'conjugation' would not have been essential — a description of the process would have been acceptable. This is a point to remember if you find yourself in that situation. You have nothing to lose by describing the process whose name you can't remember (unless the question specifically asks for the name). Candidate A scores just 1 mark as he/she doesn't mention plasmids either. Candidate B includes plasmids in his/her answer and so scores 2 marks.

> **Like all questions, this one is only easy if you know the answers, but there is really no excuse for Candidate A's poor performance (just 5 marks out of 15). There is nothing devious about any of the questions, and any candidate who had revised the topic thoroughly should be able to equal Candidate B's score of 10. If you do not know the material, you cannot hope to score the marks.**

Mitosis and tumour formation

Scientists collected data on the most common cancers in men and women in the UK. The results are shown in the table.

Site (men)	% of all cancers (men)
Lung	21
Skin	14
Prostate	10
Bladder	5
Colon	6
Stomach	5
Rectum	5
Lymph nodes	3
Oesophagus	2
Pancreas	2
Other cancers	27

Site (women)	% of all cancers (women)
Breast	19
Skin	11
Lung	8
Colon	6
Stomach	3
Ovary	3
Cervix	3
Rectum	3
Uterus	2
Bladder	2
Other cancers	40

(a) (i) The data suggest that there are more cancers of the lung in men than in women. This is not necessarily the case. Explain why. (2 marks)

(ii) Suggest and explain two reasons why the incidence of skin cancer appears to be higher in men than in women. (4 marks)

(b) The tumour suppressor gene p53 is mutated in many human cancer cells. Scientists are trying to find ways of repairing the damaged gene. In one trial, they are using altered viruses to carry normal p53 genes into cancer cells. The treatment has shown promising results in laboratory animals.

(i) Why would introducing normal p53 genes into the cancer cells be an effective way of treating the cancer? (3 marks)

(ii) Give scientific reasons why the use of laboratory animals in this research may not be justified. (2 marks)

(iii) The use of viruses to deliver the p53 gene in humans may not be effective. Suggest two reasons why. (4 marks)

Total: 15 marks

Candidates' answers to question 10

Candidate A

(a) (i) Because we don't know how many cancers there are.

Candidate B

(a) (i) It does not tell us how many cancers there were in men and women. If there were a lot more cancers in women then 8% could give a bigger number than 21% in men.

> ✍ Candidate A does not make clear that he/she is talking about all cancers. Candidate B finally makes this clear and then correctly relates percentages to possible numbers. Candidate A scores no marks while Candidate B scores 2.

Candidate A

(a) (ii) Men could spend longer in the sun and could also not look after their skin as well as women.

Candidate B

(a) (ii) Prolonged sunbathing could result in sunburn which could lead to cancers forming. Also they may be more at risk because of where they work.

> ✍ Both correctly identify sunburn as a risk factor, which only Candidate B explains adequately. Candidate A's suggestion of 'not looking after their skin' is far too vague to be credited. Candidate B tries to identify a second factor, but it too is too imprecise to be credited. Candidate A scores 1 mark, Candidate B scores 2.

Candidate A

(b) (i) The normal p53 gene would stop the cancer developing further.

Candidate B

(b) (i) The p53 gene is a tumour suppressor gene. Genes like this stop or slow down the development of a tumour. So putting the normal gene into cancer cells would stop them dividing.

> ✍ Candidate A has scored only 1. If there are 3 marks available (as here) you cannot hope to score full marks if you just write a one-line answer. Candidate B clearly describes the function of tumour suppressor genes and how they achieve this, but doesn't really make clear that the inserted gene would restore the normal function of the gene, lost by the mutation. Candidate B scores 2 marks.

Candidate A

(b) (ii) The animals may suffer because they are made to develop cancers. Also, because they are different from humans, the results may not help us much.

Candidate B

(b) (ii) Mice are a different species and so may respond differently to the treatment.

> ✍ Candidate A begins by giving an emotional response, but does go on to give a reasoned answer by identifying the fact that the laboratory animals are different

10
question

species from humans. However, the phrase 'may not help us much' is too vague, even though, in the context it is written it may mean 'animals respond differently'. You cannot expect an examiner to interpret your answers for you. The onus is on you to communicate your answers clearly. Candidate B scores 2 marks for a clear answer, whereas Candidate A scores just 1.

Candidate A
(b) (iii) The viruses may not be able to get into the cells and the immune system may destroy them.

Candidate B
(b) (iii) The viruses may be unable to enter the cells and so the gene would not be delivered. They might not release the gene once in the cell.

Both candidates make the obvious point that the viruses may not be able to enter the cells, and Candidate B explains the consequences of this. Neither really makes the point that the gene may not be activated, although Candidate B comes close by saying it may not be released. An examiner may well decide that this is effectively the same as saying the gene cannot enter. Candidate A scores just 1 mark and Candidate B scores 2.

Candidate A scores just 4 marks out of 15. This is largely a result of not supplying the detail and giving answers that are just too vague. You must try to use scientific language wherever possible, and at least make your answers clear. If in doubt, an examiner will mark a poorly expressed answer wrong. You must communicate clearly with the examiner. Candidate B does this, but also fails to supply detail on some occasions, scoring 10 marks out of 15.

In all the questions Candidate B has performed better than Candidate A. On several occasions, Candidate A clearly understands the biology required in the answers, but does not supply the detail. You cannot hope to be awarded 5 marks for a couple of lines.

Make sure that you:
- **note the verb used: are you being asked to describe, explain or analyse?**
- **take careful note of the subject of the question, and of any qualification (e.g. for how long, between which times?)**
- **tailor your answers to these criteria**

On several occasions, Candidate A has been too imprecise in his/her wording. The examiner will be reasonable and if your answer is clearly saying the same as the mark scheme in a slightly different way, you will not be penalised. However, the examiner is not clairvoyant and if your answer is not clear, you will not be credited with any marks. The onus is on you to communicate your answer clearly.

Finally, do not write more than you have to. If a question is only allocated 1 mark, do not write a paragraph just because you know all about that topic.